The Eightfold Kingdom Within

The Eightfold Kingdom Within

CAROL ROBINSON'S
COLLECTED WORKS

Essays on the Beatitudes and the Gifts of the Holy Ghost

CAROL JACKSON ROBINSON
Foreword by Rev. Fr. James Doran
Introduction by Gregorio Montejo, PhD

AROUCA PRESS

First Published by
Ave Maria Press, Notre Dame, IN (1962-1963)
Used with the permission of Ave Maria Press
2019 © by Arouca Press
Foreword © Fr. James H. Doran
Introduction © Gregorio Montejo

All rights reserved:
No part of this book may be reproduced or transmitted,
in any form or by any means, without permission
ISBN 978-1-9994729-9-3

Arouca Press
PO Box 55003
Bridgeport PO
Waterloo, ON N2J3G0
Canada
www.aroucapress.com
Send inquiries to info@aroucapress.com

Book design and cover by Michael Schrauzer
Cover:
The Beatitudes, St. Margaret's Church, Rottingdean, East Sussex
Produced by Mayer & Co. of Munich, c. 1870

CONTENTS

	Editor's Note	vii
	Foreword	ix
	Introduction	xiii
1	The Christian is a Happy Fool	1
2	Blessed are the Poor in Spirit	7
3	Blessed are the Meek	15
4	By the Waters of Babylon	23
5	The Saint, The Crackpot and the Secular Social Reformer	31
6	Enlightened Self-Interest	39
7	20/20 Spiritual Vision	47
8	World Without End	55
9	Pie in the Sky	63
10	The Poor in Spirit	71
11	The Meek	89

EDITOR'S NOTE

THE NINE ESSAYS THAT BEGIN THIS BOOK were originally published as a series titled "Eight Keys to the Kingdom" in the *Ave Maria* magazine for nine consecutive weeks (February 24–April 21) in 1962 as part of a Lenten series on the beatitudes and the gifts of the Holy Ghost. The subsequent two works, *The Poor in Spirit*, and *The Meek*, included as chapters 10 and 11, were small pamphlets written in 1963 with a similar theme.

This book is the second in Carol Robinson's *Collected Works* series. Her penetrating analysis of the modern world show the fruit of a mind absorbed in the thought of St. Thomas Aquinas—her life-long companion. We hope that these essays will help Catholics understand how the Faith has importance for the totality of their lives.

Grateful acknowledgement is given to Ave Maria Press for permission to republish this material. Additional thanks is extended to Fr. James Doran and Gregorio Montejo for their invaluable contributions.

FOREWORD

CHRISTIANITY, WHEN IT IS ORTHODOX, IS A religion of the heart, but not one of sentimentality. Catholicism in all its tradition has been a religion illuminating the mind so that the spirit might find dwelling with God.

Confusion and discomfort: this is the prospect of embracing the Gospel in the modern world. Add to these the incomprehension or enmity from others, and you have a potent source of discouragement to living an integral and integrated Catholic life today.

Must it be so?

The Good One of course remains ever the same in charity and omnipotence, so the root and source of all holiness is still sound. The unknown factor then must lie in the hearts of men if Christianity is to be put into action. There will always be some—"the world"—who will consistently resist the grace and action of the Almighty. Holding this book, it must be otherwise with us. Faith has been given, grace has taken root, and so must the flourishing of fidelity and holiness. Is this the happiness we seek?

These small essays lay out considerations from the early 1960s, from a moment of time that was to launch a tsunami of confusion such as the world has rarely seen. We benefit from hindsight, but not from the structure of a society and culture that still held in mid-twentieth century. Even in its compromised form post-World War II, it was more sound than that in which we find ourselves. Lamenting is unacceptable as we know well that the Hidden God of majesty supplies the help necessary to each individual appropriate to his life and in accord with the requirements of his time. And ours is a time in desperate need of grace and holiness. Faithful, we rely on the goodness of God to supply what is wanting to us to live according to His Divine Heart.

Thus, confidence and determination should be the watchwords as we plow through the modern muck of murky thought.

This confidence is not from us, but relies on the power of the Most High.

We have to let go all purely human calculation as we follow with our crosses behind the Lord, and the Beatitudes do just that. They crash through the hesitancy, the timidity, the machinations, which paralyze so much of what could be good in our lives. We ignore the Lord too often, turn back and do the "reasonable" thing, but a thing which Our Lord had called the "dead burying the dead". "Being reasonable", a thing so many think they know, but in reality misunderstand, and in misunderstanding they labor to justify *their* "interpretation" of "how things should be". Pure illusion is all of this, and, ego-centric, contrary to the integrity of the Gospel of Christ. The Beatitudes shatter these illusions.

A man cannot not *choose* his own happiness. We originate from Infinite Goodness and we are sealed by that fundamental orientation to return to Goodness. The key is what we think to be goodness. Power? Sex? Money? Affluence? More stuff? We surf life like a child rolling around in one those arcade games filled with plastic balls that one "swims through". While we loll around amidst much "stuff" during life, there is only one thing that can bring to rest the human heart: the Infinite Goodness from which it came. We cannot not choose our own happiness, but we CAN choose to be deceived by many little goods that tickle our fancy during our days here below.

This is why the Beatitudes crash into us. Far from being a pretty example of framed embroidery and poetry, the Beatitudes, when considered fully, upend everything. It is impossible to imagine what must have been the reaction of the people hearing these statements for the first time. Habituated to them, we easily become indifferent to them. Ponder them, and they will ignite. Pray on them, and they will explode. Assimilate them and they will turn a person inside out — freeing him from the illusory sources of "happiness" to which he had clung up to that point.

This reworking of human life is the remedy to confusion and discomfort, because confusion is the result of faulty thinking, and discomfort derives from the illusion that what one possesses is supposed to make for happiness. So modern man plods on in darkness, clinging to ephemeral things, thinking he is "happy", but knowing, better yet, experiencing it really isn't so. It makes us all angry. This is why we have become a nation of addicts and lonely people.

How is it that so many are surprised that *loneliness* and *addiction* (to whatever) afflict a multitude in this world of make-believe where we find ourselves? They call it an "epidemic", but epidemics originate in external things, it is from viruses that infection sets in. Illusion, anger, addiction, and rage are not external viruses that we "catch". These are not pathogens we have caught, but interior rot from muddled choices. Focused as we have been on material things, we have for generations neglected the human heart and That for Which it was created. We now die of loneliness, addiction, and despair, but only long after the heart has been smothered and the spirit atrophied.

The Beatitudes act as a defibrillator to these lethal conditions, should we choose to listen. They re-animate the soul by enkindling charity and warmth within a heart that has grown cold. And everyone knows that without a healthy heart one eventually dies for good.

Rev. Fr. James Doran
Waterville, Maine
July 4, 2019

INTRODUCTION

AS EXPOUNDED IN THE SERMON ON THE Mount, the Beatitudes are at once a summation of the vicissitudes to be overcome by those who strive to follow Christ and a promise of everlasting happiness to those who overcome the challenges of living an authentic Christian life. Early Christians, such as Augustine and Ambrose, began to draw connections between these injunctions, meant to lead the believer to the Kingdom of God, with the Gifts of the Holy Spirit as first enumerated in a Messianic oracle by the prophet Isaiah (Isa. 11:1-3): "And the spirit of the Lord shall rest upon him: the spirit of wisdom, and of understanding, the spirit of counsel, and of fortitude, the spirit of knowledge, and of godliness. And he shall be filled with the spirit of the fear of the Lord." According to Aquinas, such Gifts are necessary because acquired human virtues perfect "man according as it is natural for him to be moved by his reason in his interior and exterior actions" (*ST* I-II, q.68, a.1). However, there are supernatural perfections to which we are called that can only be achieved if we are "disposed to be moved by God in a divine way" (Ibid). Hence, these perfections are called Gifts, "not only because God infuses them gratuitously, but also because by them man is disposed to be made readily moveable by divine inspiration" (Ibid). Thus, the Beatitudes are not merely an eschatological hope, a promise of happiness to be fulfilled at some distant point in the future, but a mode of being empowered by God's grace that presents us with the ability to live increasingly God-shaped lives. They are, as Carol Robinson will explain, the Holy Spirit "acting in us, as He sees fit, and with all the resources of the divinity, in such a way that we too act, "but secondarily—consenting, rejoicing, continuously acknowledging that we could never do it on our own, and giving thanks."

In his commentary on the Sermon on the Mount, Augustine had begun to explicate the close affinities between the Beatitudes and the Gifts, and to indicate how in tandem they trace out a progressive ascent in holiness, with a pious fear of the Lord at the base of this ascent and divine wisdom at its glorious summit (*De Sermone Domini in Monte*, I, 4) As Augustine explains, this life-long spiritual itinerary can also be understood as a period of purification, encompassing an initial phase of active practice of virtues associated with the Gifts of piety, fortitude, knowledge, and counsel. This is followed by a stage where the Gifts of understanding, fortitude, and charity prepare us for our final consummation. In Aquinas' description, this highest form of human delight is to be found in the beatific vision, the intellect's contemplation of the essence of God as perfected by the ineffable joy that it produces in the believer — a union of heart and mind promised by Christ in the Beatitude "Blessed are the pure in heart, for they shall see God" (Matt. 5:8) — indeed, they will be united so intimately to the Lord that they will be called children of God (5:9).

This last dominical promise of blessedness gives us a further indication of how in the Angelic Doctor's theology the Beatitudes, which appropriates the Augustinian correlation between Beatitudes and Gifts but expands upon it, these elements are organically related in such a way that they allow us to participate in the divine life of God. In Thomas' system, the Gifts predispose us and prepare us to receive the promptings of the Spirit (*ST* I-II, q. 68), while the Beatitudes are seen as the active response to those promptings, an ongoing participation through God's gracious Gift in His divine attributes that renders us spiritually fruitful (*ST* I-II, qq. 69-70). Thus, for example, the Gift of knowledge allows us to see creation from God's point of view, blesses us with the ability to mourn for our sins and those of others, fortifies us with the infused virtue of faith, and finally rewards us with the fruit of fealty to God and His commandments (*ST* II-II, q. 9).

The remainder of the Gifts operate in a similarly interrelated manner. The Gift of fear instils in us a reverent dread of displeasing God, reorders our concupiscible appetites, our desiring emotions, blesses us as "poor in spirit" and thus able to deprecate lower goods and come to experience God as our highest good, thereby fostering the virtue of temperance for earthly things and a hope in achieving God as our final eternal end as the fruition of temporal self-control (*ST* II-II, q. 19). The Gift of piety inspires us to revere God in blessed meekness as our Father in heaven and to look upon our neighbors as His fellow children in Christ, inculcates the virtue of justice which allows us to have a right relationship with both God and neighbor, thereby ultimately bequeathing to us the fruits of generosity of spirit and gentleness of demeanor (*ST* II-II, q. 121). The Gift of fortitude allows us to face the trials and tribulations of this earthly existence with the virtue of holy courage, blesses us with an unquenching appetite even through the most daunting challenges for divine justice, and yields a culminating harvest of long-suffering patience (*ST* II-II, q. 139). The crowning Gift of the active life, counsel, grants us the ability to grasp by means of the virtue of prudence what is the correct course of action to undertake in a particular time and place, under a particular set of circumstances, even if what God wishes us to do is contrary to what the world wants (*ST* II-II, q. 52). Oftentimes, God counsels us to render mercy unto those who are despised or ignored by earthly powers, or those who have wronged us in some way; hence the Beatitude tells us that "Blessed are the merciful, for they shall obtain mercy." The attendant fruit of heeding God's merciful counsel is a state of beneficent generosity.

With the Gift of understanding, we shift our focus to the contemplative life, wherein we perfect our capacity to know and to love that which is most knowable and most lovable, God. Understanding perfects our speculative intellect, our aptitude to know the truth of things (*ST* II-II, q.8). However, this is no mere abstract, discursive knowledge of God as the source of transcendent truth, but rather a more experiential form of coming to know that unites us to the object of our knowledge.

This Gift's matching beatitude is Christ's promise that "blessed are they who mourn, for they shall be comforted." Which is to say, by means of this Gift we learn to piously mourn the fact that God is not yet fully present to us in this life (*ST* II-II, q. 9). In an act of comprehensive knowing, that which is known comes to be in the intellect in the mode of the knower. Or, as Thomas helpfully explains in regard to our knowledge of the divine, "When any created intellect sees the essence of God, the essence of God itself becomes the intelligible form of the intellect" (*ST* I, q.12, a.5). This sort of knowledge finds complete fruition only in the eschatological vision of God's essence enjoyed by the blessed in heaven since it is not possible for a created intellect to achieve such illumination by its unaided powers in this life. It is an illuminative capacity bestowed upon the intellect by divine grace, and according to Aquinas, "by this light the blessed are made deiform—that is, like to God" (Ibid: *secundum hoc lumen efficiuntur deiformes, id est Deo similes*).

Finally, the Gift of wisdom perfects the human will, by which we love the God we have come to know as our supreme good. By virtue of an augmentingly ardent love for God, our disordered affections are progressively purified, and as a result, we begin to experience God's sweetness (*ST* II-II, q. 45). That is to say, we commence to enjoy an ever-more profoundly intimate knowledge of God, rooted in an abiding love, by which we taste and savor divine things, as the Latin term *sapientia*, wisdom, which is closely aligned to the verb *sapere*, to savor, clearly intimates. Its complementary beatitude, "Blessed are the peacemakers, for they shall be called the sons of God," attunes us to the fact that the fruit of such a union will be the surpassing peace and joy of being adopted children of God and thus perfectly remade in the Father's image. This inexpressible beatitude can only be obtained, as Thomas relates, by a "kind of participation of the Godhead, about which it is written (2 Pet 1:4) that by Christ we are made partakers of the Divine nature" (*ST* I-II, q.62, a.1). To be sure, by such divine means a bond is established, a relationship of ecstatic love that "makes the beloved to be in the lover, and vice versa," a placing outside of ourselves or blissful transport that radically and eternally unites us to the God (*ST* I-II, q.28, a.2).

Carol Jackson Robinson's *Eightfold Kingdom Within* is a noteworthy attempt to communicate Thomas' developed thought of the Beatitudes to a non-academic audience, and while she does eschew any discussion of the intricacies of doctrinal development, subjects of undoubted interest to the historical theologians, nonetheless her series of remarkable articles reveal that Robinson was a careful and highly insightful reader of Aquinas. Over the course of her essays, Robinson rightly focuses on the task of placing the Beatitudes and their attendant Gifts once again at the center of Christian spiritual life. Perhaps Robinson's insightfulness is most evident in the way she grasps that for Thomas, and indeed for much of the Christian tradition both East and West, the purpose and aim of the spiritual life is deification, what she refers to as the ongoing process of "being supernaturalized." Moreover, Robinson stresses that this process of conversion, of becoming progressively more deiform, perforce requires our adoption as earthly children of the heavenly Father. If truth be told, that the process cannot proceed at all unless, like obedient children, we meekly receive the divine instigation of the Spirit, for only in this manner will we be established "firmly in the family of God our Father."

Along with Aquinas, Robinson recapitulates the requisite ascending steps through the Beatitudes and Gifts of the active life towards the heights of the contemplative life. Robinson bracingly argues that there can be no approach to the most exalted reaches of spirituality without an often-painful traversal through the vagaries of quotidian activity. Recognizing that the vast majority of her secular audience would find themselves seemingly mired in these earliest stages, she emphasizes that it is precisely the "painful yet sanctifying effects of the active life" that allow us to make progress. It is in such passages, often illustrated with effective anecdotes from contemporary society, that Robison most successfully takes the somewhat abstruse theme of the Beatitudes out of the rarified province of the mystics and scholars of ascetical theology, and places it squarely where it most desperately needs to be, at the very heart of the average Christian man and woman in their everyday struggle to achieve holiness.

Robinson is even more astute in the way she makes the contemplative apex of the spiritual itinerary traced out by Thomas easily relatable to the common reader. As it turns out, the pitfalls and promises of the contemplative life are no longer of crucial importance only to contemplatives. Undoubtedly influenced by her favorite Thomistic commentator—Réginald Marie Garrigou-Lagrange, OP—Robinson boldly connects the Gift of understanding as the perfection of the human intellect in its encounter with God with the dark night of the soul as elaborated by St. John of the Cross. In works such as *The Three Ages of the Interior Life*, Garrigou-Lagrange had constructed a grand synthesis of spiritual theology, writing that the "teaching of St. John of the Cross . . . fully conforms to what is said of the beatitudes in the Gospel, and to the way St. Augustine and St. Thomas understood them" (Vol. I, p. 194). Building upon this premise, the "Sacred Monster of Thomism" as he came to be called for his unstintingly rigorous interpretation of Thomist doctrine, elucidates a quite close connection between the final contemplative Beatitudes, the Spirit's Gifts of understanding and wisdom, and the purificatory climax of that perforce all Christian are called to endure before they can enjoy the beatific vision. Garrigou-Lagrange's message is breathtaking in its clarifying directness: "very few Christians would reach perfection" without the aid of this grace of temporal purgation (Ibid). Hence, Christians must pray to arrive at the Beatitudes of contemplation, which proceeds from faith tested by the sorrows of the mind and the heart endemic to a fallen creation, yet nonetheless enlightened by the Gifts of the Holy Ghost.

Carol Robinson is particularly eloquent in her account of the passive purification of the senses as well as the sufferings of spiritual aridity that accompany this period of purification that must be undergone in order to arrive at our beatific destiny—to become, in Robinson's own words, "quasi-divinized." The "awful darkness" of purgation, she assures us, is the "effect of too much light." It simultaneously blinds and burns us "in one final terrible purification;" the believer must, therefore, be blackened and made hideous before being "transformed into the fire itself." Elaborating upon the teaching of the Common Doctor, Robinson highlights the integrative nature of this purgative transformation. While the Gift of understanding has rendered our "highest faculty"—the intellect—subject to God, our affective union with God takes place in a will transfigured through the love of God, the fruition of the culminating Gift of wisdom.

> The union has taken place in the will: his will with God's Will, through charity, because he now loves God wholly through the subjection of his most resistant part, his mind. Deep, deep in his soul, to which he now can penetrate in prayer, he is aware of a Presence Whom he can "touch," and in "touching," knows. This is contemplation. Penetrating, blinding, delightful, ineffable.

While the obscurity of faith remains our common lot in this life, where we cannot see God face to face, divine wisdom nonetheless leads the faithful through the darkness of the intellect, so that "when the Holy Ghost has completed His work of transforming them into children of God," when the Gift of "Wisdom has given them the highest glimpse possible in this life of the plan of Holy Wisdom," they have been led to the very threshold of the beatific vision.

Gregorio Montejo, PhD
Assistant Professor of Historical Theology
Boston College
September 3, 2019

1

The Christian is a Happy Fool

BEGINNING A NEW SERIES ON THE BEATITUDES
AND THEIR MEANING IN THE DAILY LIVES
OF CATHOLICS IN AMERICA IN 1962...

A FEW YEARS AGO A PROMINENT CATHolic wrote a book in praise of our times. He said we had made amazing progress in the last 400 years. He pointed to the enormous increase in wealth. He praised democracy for allowing serfs to become millionaires within a generation. He spoke of the education available to all. He noted the disappearance of cruel instruments of torture in our prisons and of the universal compassion felt for the sick, the unfortunate and the needy, to such an extent that we make the welfare of all the first responsibility of the state. Never before in history, as he pointed out, has there been such a passion for social justice. On the material side, the forces of production have been brought to such a pinnacle of perfection that the masses of people can live far above the level of decency. We might add that the new horizons of space exploration point to new heights of human achievement beyond the imagination.

Be all that as it may, the thoughtful man will pause before the spectacle of man's progress. "Four hundred years," he will say to himself, "that means all our brilliant modern achievements have taken place in the era of de-Christianization. As Christ was pushed out of government, business, education, welfare work, law, social life, conversation, and indeed every area of living, things have gotten better. There seems to be an unmistakable inverse ratio between progress and the influence of Christ. How come?"

The usual answer goes like this: "Yes, we've made lots of progress in other fields, but we haven't gone ahead so fast spiritually. We have to catch up spiritually. Because of negligence in the religious department of our life our other progress is itself in jeopardy. We simply can't have so much divorce, insanity, alcoholism, juvenile delinquency, etc."

This is a pretty lame answer, since it concedes all the premises of secularism. It is willing to grant that religion is a separate department of life, personal and interior; that we can get along much better without it in public affairs; and that it cannot command the enthusiasm of the most brilliant and dedicated people.

The Marxist answer is more convincing: We have simply outgrown Christianity. It is a religion which is not true in itself, but which served very well in a more primitive economy. Religion is not a private affair, and it can build civilizations. Christianity built the medieval civilization, which was full of beauty, happiness and order. But the world is evolving through changes in the modes of production. We have not only outgrown Christianity, but also the need for any religion. Man himself is now a sort of god. He is establishing a new humanistic order of society and he will soon change man himself through the new social and medical sciences. Alcoholism, insanity, juvenile delinquency and other such sources of unhappiness are simply an inevitable accompaniment of the decadent and transitional post-Christian period.

Our thoughtful man will be shaken by our analysis. He will remember that Christ said: "Without Me, you can do nothing," and he will look for an explanation from the Christian camp which is confident, comprehensive and convincing.

For that explanation, we must first see contemporary society in Christian focus.

It will be a help, by way of analogy, to look at the way conscientious non-believers rear their children.

A new baby comes. Our non-believing parents do not see it as a gift from God. They do not rush off to get it baptized. They do not teach it to worship. They do not train it in virtue, pointing out what is good and what is bad. They do not see it as their sacred duty to start this child on a journey which will end in heaven.

Nevertheless, they are conscientious parents. They want the

best for their child. But what is the best?

They look to the child to find out. What are the greatest heights to which this child can climb? What are its potentialities? Is it a pretty girl? Then she must be directed toward popularity. Or marrying well. Or if exceptionally pretty, she must become Miss Rheingold or Miss America. They will make the necessary sacrifices to set off her beauty by good clothes all along the line. Or perhaps it is a boy with a gift for music, or football, or physics. Then these are the lines of concentrated exploitation. Well, you get the idea.

Something similar happened to Western civilization as it shed its Christianity. We did briefly in the 13th century have a civilization impregnated by grace and centered on Christ. At least the order of society was ruled by Christian norms.

During the last centuries society has progressively withdrawn from these norms. One department of life after another has been freed to see what it could make of itself. So, for instance, laissez-faire capitalism was simply the freedom of all men to make as much money as possible. In the nature of things it was an uneven contest, of course. So we got the impresarios of big business, whose wealth was spectacular. So were their material empires, and sometimes their philanthropies, and above all the disorders which followed in the wake of their conquests.

But it wasn't only business. It was a virtuoso civilization all the way around, and still is. Whatever man can do, he has done, whether it is hitting high C, splitting the atom, or reaching the moon. We have had no other purpose these many years past except to show how clever we are. We are very clever. So are devils. And as every single thing has been done to excess because there were no limits to contain it, the disorders mounted.

Our contemporary world is full of absurd contrasts, and related contrasts. Armies of doctors are working for a cancer cure while nobody talks about death, although men are going to die anyhow even if they are cured of cancer. Miss America can't manage a successful life-long career as Mrs. Smith. Television is electronically wonderful, while its programs are childish. We have drastically reduced the infant mortality rate, while criminal abortions are soaring into the millions. We talk about brotherhood while making hydrogen bombs.

It is many years since Leo XIII said of factories that material goods come out of them perfected, while men come out of them degraded. The same thing can now be said of the whole world; the more comprehensive and efficient becomes its technological and scientific organization, the closer men themselves come to some form of monstrous impersonal and total slavery.

Now the root cause of all our difficulties is that we have cut loose from God and from God's order. All things betray us because we have betrayed Him. It is not because we are unconcerned about man, but because we don't know what a man is for. Like the unbelieving parents, we try to work things out according to our own ideas.

So the root remedy is humility. We may as well confess that all our splendid achievements add up to a kind of nothingness. They haven't made us happy, and they will end up by destroying us. Let's do an about-face and try things God's way.

We begin at the end, and the instruction is clear: "Be ye perfect as your heavenly Father is perfect."

That's reassuring. It is our own perfection that we are to worry about. However difficult that may be, at least we can get the world off our shoulders for awhile. We don't have to live through every summit conference as though it really mattered what we thought.

Neither do we have to wait until after the dictatorship of the proletariat before we begin to improve.

This perfection for which we are destined is a supernatural perfection, which means that it is not causally dependent on a good society or a bad society, which is reassuring too, in view of the present state of affairs. Presently we will see that the dependence is the other way around: A good society is the result of the internal transformation of men, and not an immediate result either. The workings of grace in the soul are instantaneous (as in the sacraments), but the effects of grace on our resisting human natures takes a long time, and on society still longer.

But what does it mean to be perfect as our heavenly Father is perfect? Does it mean that we are going to be pure spirits? Or that we are going to be omnipotent? Or that we are going to know everything before it happens?

Obviously not. But it must mean something. Consider Christ. He was perfect man and also perfect God. Furthermore, as the Word of God, He is the perfect reflection of the Father. We are supposed to be "other Christs," so that must mean that we are supposed to be images of the Image of the Father.

Theologians say that it is the Holy Ghost Who makes us perfect. He formed Christ in Mary's womb, and He forms Christ in us. In good times and in bad times. Whether we have an atomic war or we don't. Of course we have to work along with Him and this co-operation will partly be in function of our times, but if we are docile, even our weakness and our degradation are not a barrier to His action.

How does He do it?

He works from the inside of the inside. He dwells in the center of the soul. That center is a kind of control tower governing all the operations of the person whose soul it is. We are sitting at the controls. If we are in a state of grace the Holy Ghost is there too (so is the entire Trinity, but His is especially the work of sanctification), and we have a whole set of new and elevated equipment for directing our lives to union with God in heaven. This parallels and perfects the old equipment in the course of its superior operations. All this new equipment belongs to the Holy Ghost, even though we are still sitting at the controls. It is almost as though He helps us, although of course He is more powerful than we are. His powers are sort of limited by the human channels through which it must pass.

However, in addition to the above, we are given some other and very special equipment, which in a way belongs to us because it is there all the time, as long as we do not lose charity; but only the Holy Ghost can operate it. This special equipment is known as the gifts of the Holy Ghost. It is sort of like a keyboard which enables the Holy Ghost to draw upon the omnipotence and the omniscience and the other divine powers to guide and direct our lives. But when He does this, He is sitting at the controls, while we cooperate as readily as possible in a subordinate role.

It is when the Holy Ghost takes over the controls with some sort of regularity that we start being perfect as our heavenly Father is perfect, and it is when He is there almost continuously that we reach the summit of Christian perfection in this life.

Christ has told us exactly what the Christian is like who has reached this final stage of perfection and fruitfulness. You will find the most complete description in St. Matthew's Gospel, starting with the 25th verse of the fourth chapter, and finishing with the 13th verse of the fifth chapter.

What is he like, this ideal Christian?

He is a fool.

He really is a fool. He loves poverty. He is meek. He looks at this nice world and weeps. He hungers and thirsts (for which don't read "organizes and pickets") for justice. He is merciful, on a non-selective basis. He is clean of heart, and not necessarily "gone" on hygiene. He is a peacemaker who starts with his own soul. And he gets persecuted for his trouble.

Oh, yes, and he is also the happiest of men.

Do you doubt the power of this fool to transform the world? Try it.

"Hath not God made foolish the wisdom of this world?...

For the foolishness of God is wiser than men: and the weakness of God is stronger than men.

"But the foolish things of the world hath God chosen, that he may confound the wise."

2

Blessed are the Poor in Spirit

*"Blessed are the poor in spirit, for theirs
is the kingdom of heaven." (Matt. 5: 3)*

THERE IS A VERY COMMON MISTAKE THAT is made about the beatitudes. People suppose that because they represent the summits of Christian living they are only for an elite. According to this view, you are disqualified to begin with if you are a lay person (after all, you are not leading a life of perfection, and they are perfection), and doubly disqualified if you live, as we all do, in a materialistic society in which it is next to impossible to make ends meet, much less to rise to spiritual heights.

But the beatitudes are the action of the Holy Ghost in us. If we are baptized and in a state of grace, He is present in our souls, and so are the seven gifts which facilitate His action. He can use them whenever He wishes, and there are two situations which evoke His action. One is the invitation of a soul which has done all it can to make way for his action by asceticism and prayer; and the other is a Christian in a tight spot. As an example of the latter, we are told quite plainly in the Gospel that the Holy Ghost will put words in our mouths when we are hauled before the judges of the world, and it is not just saintly Christians who are liable to need this sort of help.

Let's face it. Most of us are going to qualify for the action of the Holy Ghost by being in a tight spot. Two ways. Some of us are personal failures, whose desperate plight is more or less our own. Like Francis Thompson, who was a dope addict. Like the alcoholics. Then there's the generality of us, who are still fighting a losing battle in a society which makes it harder and harder to keep the law of Christ.

Keeping this emergency principle in mind, let us examine the first beatitude: *Blessed are the poor in spirit, for theirs is the kingdom of heaven.*

To be poor in spirit means to be detached from worldliness, from material possessions and honors. Of course there are degrees of detachment, and so of poverty of spirit, but the fullness of the beatitude is contained in Christ's advice to the rich young man: "Go sell all thou hast and give to the poor, and come follow me."

You can see the problem immediately. The typical modern young person doesn't have anything, or at least not anything substantial. He has some take-home pay which never seems to stretch far enough. He has social security, unemployment insurance and Blue Cross, but these are not negotiable and the poor have them better. For the rest he has luxurious consumer goods which he is paying for on time, and credit cards. In other words, he has the precarious use of the gadget home, a fancy car, maybe even a swimming pool or a boat, while he can keep up the payments, and mountain of debts. Meanwhile he and his wife and children are under fantastic pressure to move to yet higher levels of conspicuous consumption, status, and indebtedness.

I know a charming and soft-hearted young man who landed a job as salesman in sure-fire scheme of mass landscaping of suburban housing developments. He was to go from door to door selling shrubbery on time, according to plans A, B and C. Because he really was soft-hearted, he quit after two days. One after another of the pert little housewives in the just-finished ranch houses had cried on his shoulder about the mire of her family's indebtedness, so instead of selling anything he was in danger of handling over his own few remaining dollars.

These little families—the typical young American family now—are sort of indentured servants. So far from having a nest egg of property or money which protects their independence, they have already spent the money which they must now earn. This puts them at the mercy of their creditors, the banks and loan companies, but as the welfare state develops it will be the government which gains increasing power over them. As long as the present commercial orientation lasts, so will the overwhelming temptations to luxury living continue, because the credit schemes and advertising which make it so easy and so tempting to buy what we need like a hole in our head and what can only estrange us farther from spiritual realities, are essential instruments of a cancerous economic system. They have to create a demand, never mind how artificial it is, for machine output which must accelerate or collapse, and for a systematic and accelerating exploitation of all natural resources and scientific developments.

There is no point here in retracing the follies of our prodigal civilization by which we have arrived at this unhappy, unstable and unhealthy penultimate situation. Our problem is to see it in spiritual perspective, and in that perspective things look pretty desperate. Even the secularist, with his practically uninstructed conscience, is like a greyhound chasing an ever-receding rabbit of economic stability. The Catholic has the additional "handicap" of the natural and moral law. For him, on the face of it, having another child usually spells disaster. And not having another child spells another kind of disaster.

It is in such a society, then, that we are invited to be poor in spirit. The question is: How?

The first step, surely, is to forget about the rich young man. One does hear of rich young men, scions of mercantile empires, for instance, who disdain their inheritances to enter the Trappists. Good. Most of us are not like that. Most of us would improve our material lot by entering a third order regular, and this not because the religious live as luxuriously as we do, but because they have security, which is the priceless commodity of our time.

The next thing is to look carefully and cynically at the rational use of material things. Theoretically this is where we should begin; by using creatures well, which most of us don't. We should aim at the balanced budget, the savings account, the well-laid plans for future contingencies, including the college education of our spaced offspring. We should reduce our expenditures to a modest outlay consonant with our state of life.

Some few people will be able to follow this rational plan. They are the ones who get off to a better start, or have a natural competence in the financial department, or are just lucky. Most people, however, will succeed only in devoting their entire time, thought and energy to material considerations, without in the end achieving any order by which these things can be subordinated to higher matters. The whole concept of a state in life has pretty much gone by the board in our non-functional society. Instead we have status, and status is measured by very superficial and worldly things, like a good address or the latest style clothes, or a certain model of car, or a swimming pool. Furthermore, some of our best brains and most talented artists are working night and day to persuade us to buy more and more things, and if we live in the usual manner there is no way of avoiding their blandishments, so let us not foolishly think that we ordinary people can remain unmoved.

But whether or not we pass through the well-ordered stage, the key to detachment lies elsewhere. That key is fear.

As has already been said, the beatitudes are sort of acts of the gifts of the Holy Ghost, and theologians connect each beatitude especially with a particular gift. Poverty of spirit, which is the first of the beatitudes, they connect with the lowest of the gifts, the fear of the Lord. At first this seems a bit of unnecessary synchronization, but when you start wondering how to practice the beatitude, you see that of course the gift is the clue, and its development brings us nearer to the desired summit.

We are a terrified generation, but we are afraid of the wrong things. We are afraid of losing our jobs, afraid of cancer, afraid of getting killed in an automobile accident, afraid that people won't like us, and above all afraid of insecurity, of being unable to take care of ourselves and of having no one to take care of us.

Our fear shows where our treasure is, for we fear to lose what we love. The fears of our generation indicate a desperate love of this life and our material, social and physical well-being in it. "Better Red than dead," people are beginning to say, even if only to themselves.

If, then, our fears center around sin, what a profound difference it makes! We are already living in a different dimension from that of our neighbors. We have a transcendental reference for our conduct that pierces the secular ceiling. This is true even if ours is only a servile fear that fears sin because we are afraid of going to hell, although this fear is only preliminary to that fear of the Lord which is a gift of the Holy Ghost. After all, the secular world does not believe in hell and there is a vast difference between the man who is afraid to be caught and punished here, and the man who is afraid of God's justice, which is not only more exacting, but inevitable and eternal.

We lay people twist and squirm in the secular trap. We wish we could find some way of accommodating ourselves without losing the prospect of heaven. We would like to be able to lead normal lives and *then* work our way up spiritually. But the pinch is on us increasingly, and under the circumstances this is a good thing, both for us and for the world. It will force us to reach for perfection, and somehow, later, out of that perfection, the world will be rectified.

When a person enters a religious order he skips the first couple of steps of the spiritual life. That's why, when St. John of the Cross writes for "beginners" he really means those who have already put the world behind them and are now ready to do combat with the evil in themselves at closer range.

Many of us are in a curiously similar position, though we are lay people. Our first step has to be a giant step too, and after having taken it we are dependent on God in a way that gives our life a supernatural orientation. This could be considered a sort of state of perfection.

The obvious case is that of prolific married couples. It is remarkable how a small baby or two can bring out the worst in landlords, ruin status competition and destroy the ideal of life established by the women's magazines.

Less obvious, but hard on its heels, is the plight of the teenage daughter and/or her parents, as the incompatibility between popularity and chastity grows.

But what about the conscience of the breadwinner? Let us suppose that it is by no means scrupulous. Still, one has only to read the papers to see what tremendous moral decisions have to be made in the ordinary course of business and politics. Or for that matter, college basketball. And it is rarely a choice between making an honest living and getting rich. The choice is between dishonesty and wealth or fame on the one hand; ruin on the other. And there is every likelihood that things will get worse rather than better.

We would do well to pray to Thomas More, who was a layman in a comparable spot. While he was still the king's favorite, living in a lovely house in London, he told his friends in confidence that it was unlikely any Catholics would survive the coming events with their fortune. So he must long have been prepared for the moment when his conscience forced him to resign his job as Lord Chancellor, which precipitated him into poverty. He did nothing to provoke, but patiently suffered, the subsequent loss of his lands and finally his head. While he was in prison in the Tower his wife had to sell her clothes to buy him necessities.

It could happen to us. The point is that already the choice is drastic. Not between a higher and a lower standard of living, but between taking care of ourselves, and dependence on God. The formula here is: *Seek ye first the kingdom of God and His justice, and all these things will be added unto you.* Our treasure is suddenly in heaven and our hope is in God (poverty of spirit has a close connection with the virtue of hope). Instead of being solicitous about what we will eat and wear, we must now be solicitous about pleasing God, so that in turn He will take care of us. It's like a member of AA who still is an alcoholic and who has no reservoir of temperance under his own control but who gets his sobriety minute by minute from grace.

So God takes care of us as a loving Father, directing our paths and energies as He sees fit, while our constant concern is not to be separated from Him whom we so gratefully love. Under these conditions we advance rapidly in our detachment from the goods and the honors of the world. We have a new kind of freedom; not the sort which comes of having an independent income and so not having to take any man's lip, but a real absence of covetousness. The less we want to possess things, the more we begin to appreciate creatures with the sort of appreciation St. Francis had. The sun and the moon and the stars and the birds and all the good things of the world spoke to him of God.

Those who desire the things of this world are not made happy by possessing them; only unhappy by their absence. It is God who makes men happy, but even if God is present in our souls we cannot enjoy Him while we are attached to a thousand material and physical goods. So the process of detachment brings with it not only freedom but also joy, the true light-heartedness that made St. Francis sing as he walked barefoot in the snow.

This is the kingdom of heaven within us.

3
Blessed are the Meek

"Blessed are the meek, for they shall
inherit the earth." (Matt. 5: 4)

THE CHRISTIAN IS ASKED TO BE MEEK. BUT IN
TODAY'S WORLD, CAN HE BE AND SURVIVE?

However it may have been in the past, today it is the weak who are notably not meek. The little fellows. The children. The women. The underprivileged. The poor. The workers. The prisoners. People on relief.

Of course the strong are not meek either, but it was always hard for them. Society would be pretty near perfection if the rich and the powerful and the giant intellects went about turning the other cheek. Not so with the underdogs. They have always had a very limited area in which they could safely give vent to irascibility. That is, prior to our great age of revolution.

The rebellion is now so general and so universal that we live in a kind of nightmare society, with milling mobs of people filling central squares and shouting derisively; with children solemnly sitting at round-table discussions of the President's latest foreign policy; with teenagers denouncing their parents and wives bossing their husbands; with beatniks writing blasphemous, unmetered, unpunctuated poetry, and with nations being denounced by angry young men.

Needless to say, in such an atmosphere meekness is not only conspicuous by the absence of its practice, but as an ideal it has also reached its nadir. There are even zealous Christians who would rather shout "*We* are the revolution," than hear about "Gentle Jesus, meek and mild." But of course Jesus was meek and mild and gentle, and in fact these are considered to be among the finest fruits of the operation of the Holy Ghost in our souls. So maybe we are mistaken about meekness, or about the revolution, or both. Let's investigate.

As a start, let us agree that whatever meekness is, it is not rebellion, but something very like its opposite. Then we can save definitions until later, and try to find out why it is that the rebels rebel.

Ask Candy Smith who is in Reno for divorce and remarriage (her fourth, his third) why she found life with Mr. Smith intolerable. She will note that you are more inquisitive than the courts, but may explain that their tastes in TV programs clashed.

Jim Jones, who would almost like to *kill* his parents, and boy oh boy can hardly wait until he gets out of that house for good, will be found upon investigation to have been refused the use of the family car for the high-school dance.

The rioters at the Green Hill maximum security prison are holding three guards and the prison doctor as hostages until they are promised two eggs for breakfast and an extra movie every week.

All the stevedores in London are out on strike and jeopardizing the entire economy of the British Isles because they have a vaguely uneasy feeling about the last elections.

Mrs. Joseph Kelly is training her seven children and her husband in domestic responsibilities because next week she starts working eight hours a day on the assembly line in a doughnut factory. How else will they even be able to afford a dishwashing machine and new curtains for the living room?

Mary McDowell and the other teachers at P.S. 46 have signed a petition and have threatened a stay-at-home demonstration if the gym teacher is not reinstated. He has been dismissed for making known his views on free-love and censorship in the presence of some of the students.

The little central African territory of Mumbo Jumbo is sending a special committee to the United Nations to ask immediate assistance in throwing off the yoke of the European nation to which Mumbo Jumbo is totally indebted for rescue from savagery and tribal warfare, a process well-launched but far from completion. The crisis in Mumbo Jumbo's colonialism is the result of a sharp reprimand made by the wife of a white official to an indolent native cook.

If we now go back two or three or four generations, depending on the place and the facet of life, we will find that under conditions of life which were far more severe than at present, the disposition to revolt was generally lacking, and the reasons far more substantial when the revolt did take place.

The mother who took a job was either widowed or had an incapacitated husband, and she was envied by no one.

The first divorces were allowed because of conditions which wrung the hearts of the most unfeeling judges.

If the French Revolution, which was really the parent political revolt, was not entirely necessary, at least it has been so represented to us and also was to the French populace at the time. In any case, the corruption of the officials, the duress suffered by the lowest classes and the irresponsibility of the aristocracy were far more horrible than later "imperialisms."

No 19th century American child ran away from home just because he had to get up before daybreak to light the fires and milk the cows before walking five miles to the village school.

A fastidious older friend of mine, now dead, taught school in Idaho as a young woman. She suffered all winter from bedbugs without daring to complain to the farm family with whom she was lodged, for fear of losing her job. The lodging was a major part of her salary. Otherwise she did not find the year unpleasant, although it was a one-room schoolhouse heated by a wood stove and reached by long walks through snowdrifts.

Old time nurses will tell of 20-hour days, of scrubbing the floors of long corridors and eating vile food during their training. It will also appear in the course of their reminiscences that these were among the happiest days of their lives.

These examples merely emphasize what every thinking person will have realized, that the causes of rebellion are not nowadays to be found in the concrete situation to which the rebel himself points. What is the cause then? Why are so many people bent on biting the hand that feeds them, breaking the hearts that love them, and destroying the society which sustains them, however imperfectly these things are now done?

Something can be learned form the rebel who has passed beyond the trivial excuse and who has one answer for all his shifts of jobs, changes of spouse and refusals of standards.

"*Why not?*" he will demand of you.

"Why shouldn't I go to work I want to?"

"Why shouldn't I leave the job if it doesn't please me?"

"Why do I have to write sonnets with 14 lines? Or make music that is harmonious, or bathe regularly?"

Why not indeed?

There is no compelling reason why Mrs. Smith should not divorce her third husband. But there is a reason why she shouldn't have divorced her first husband: because marriage is a bond which cannot be broken, for God made it that way. To discover firm reasons why not anything, you have to go back to the order God established or an order dependent on the order God established; in fact to the absolutes must be denied before secularism is possible.

The rebellion really began when men cast loose from the Church, for she is the guardian of God's order. It has taken all these years for the rebellion to run its course because of the retarding effects of Christian discipline and attitudes. Most men wanted to hold to the old order, or to parts of it, or to a slight breach, for pragmatic reasons. Expediency was not sufficiently compelling, especially as conditions worsened.

The rebellion has now finished its course, which was of course of destruction. The old order, God's order, has been either destroyed or perilously weakened, and this in spite of the huge presence of the Church and a huge Catholic population in places like America. Secularism has ruled out the direct Christian influence of both clerical and lay Catholics in public affairs, and as a matter of fact most of us have secular minds anyhow as a result of the general environment.

But take a good look at the plight of the rebel. Is he happy now that he has toppled a world? Does he like being totally emancipated?

No. In running away, and backing out, and rising in protest, and breaking bonds, he has simply eased himself out of whatever social order is left. He is without family, without country, without belief, without discipline, without spouse, without vocation, without training, without ties, without home, community, nest egg, without responsibilities, without convictions, without an earned reputation, without loyal, tried and trusted friends, without personal institutional loyalties of his own, without accomplishment, without virtue (that's why he lauds spontaneity), without a goal, without hope, and above all without internal peace.

This is the tired rebel, the outsider, the man whose tragedy is that he does not belong.

There are a good many tired rebels around who have nothing left but the habit of anger, who are psychologically ready to capitulate but who cannot find a place to lay down their arms.

They cannot return to their social class in a classless society. They cannot again be subject to their parents, because in theory they are adults. They cannot return to school or apprenticeship in preparation for a life now so far gone. Their marital affairs are often beyond disentangling. They cannot find use for their natural talents in a world mechanized beyond the need for personal skills and satisfactions. Neighborhoods have disappeared. How will they get to know and be known?

Theirs is not primarily a question of eating, but of belonging. If a tired rebel has money, he will probably hire a psychoanalyst to "care." If not he will easily drift into the new servility of being "cared for" at the price of a diminished life.

There is only one thing that can salvage the tired rebel, and that is heroic meekness.

A lesser meekness won't work. There is no point in telling

the rebel that he must learn to control his anger, because this passion has so developed that it fills his whole life. If he were to begin by counting to 10 before cursing the lateness of the bus, it would be like taking an aspirin tablet for a coronary.

Nor is there much point in encouraging him to submit to the circumstances in which he finds himself at the time of his willingness to surrender, on the theory that they represent the will of God for him. He knows that he has worked himself into a position in which all his circumstances are arbitrary. He does not belong in this job, or this apartment, or this town, or among these people; he has just drifted there. Unless, of course, he has himself in a trap from which there is no possible escape. In that case he does belong, as on the cross of his own crucifixion, but he has first to surrender to God.

Heroic meekness, the meekness of the beatitude, is precisely an act of belonging, for it is a fruit of the gift of piety which establishes us firmly in the family of God our Father. That is why the meek are promised the earth (and even more so heaven) as an inheritance; because God, the owner, is their Father. They are sons and heirs because Christ is their Brother. So are all other men their brothers.

The return of the rebel to the house of his Father is no perfunctory act. It is not even like the return to the sacraments of a Catholic who has fallen into mortal sin, or like an ordinary conversion. It is a total capitulation, like that of the prodigal son.

His Father has been watching afar off, from the first temper tantrum to the final failure.

"Father, I've refused the yoke a thousand times. I've messed up my life, I've wasted my talents, I've ruined my health, and now I come home bankrupt. All I want now is to do Your will, not mine. I'll start wherever You say. Just show me the first cross and I'll pick it up."

The reader is going to say that this is an extreme case. All right, it is. But there are many cases of less spectacular rebellion in which the rebel is nevertheless in a position of not belonging.

Think of the people, even with apostolic backgrounds or in the lay apostolate, who have never sunk roots and built a life because they are still trying to find out where they ought to be; whether in the convent or married, or if married, to whom, or even in what job? And of course they abound among non-Catholics, these restless people. They missed the pattern of normal growth way back. It was probably in their childhood, and probably at least nine-tenths due to the turbulence of their parents' marriages (for which the blame can be pushed back another generation, for the rebellion has been long underway). Some like the displaced persons, are simply victims of the social and moral upheaval which has climaxed the revolution.

The one segment of society which is virtually untouched by the rebellion is the private life of the Catholic Church. Religious orders and the ranks of the clergy have been quietly filled by the children of good and pious Catholic homes for generations, in disregard of the general anarchy. Now that the tide is turning, many a tired rebel wants to make his surrender at the door of a monastery or convent. This has created a kind of minor crisis because novitiates were used to building on a solid foundation. This has not made the lot of the repentant rebel any easier.

However, these misshapen lives are no problem to God, Who will cause them to bear fruit in His own way once the rebels have capitulated. As long as they try to run their own lives they can only resign themselves to some sort of semi-failure or half-loaf endured with the help of grace. If, however, they find a way of total dedication or abandonment to the will of God, with the help of a confessor or a secular institute, or in the wake of a tremendous personal catastrophe, there is no predicting what will happen. God's plans for us are always marvelous beyond our imagining, and however unemployable or undesirable we may seem and be, in worldly perspective, this is no impediment to God's realizing great things in us. Whereas if we do not relinquish control of our lives, we will be struck with our own meager plans.

But granted that these various kinds of rebels have really surrendered, and granted even that they now have a sense of belonging, how are they going to find the practical, concrete human course which will put an end to their aimless wanderings?

This way. The supreme act of meekness which constitutes the beatitude is allied not only with the gift of piety but also with the gift of counsel. They will receive from the Holy Ghost, acting through this latter gift, impulses corresponding with opportunities or suggestions from outside. Perhaps there will be sudden ideas, which will indicate not a path, but a step. It may even seem an absurd step, but as they take it they will feel peacefully sure that it is the right one. And then in the same way, another one. Like a small boy holding his father's hand and confidently going simply somewhere.

Or it may be that the rebel has all too clear a path to follow, for it may lead back to those responsibilities which he evaded and the crosses he refused. In that case he will depend heavily on the gift of fortitude, which is also allied to meekness.

"Learn of me, for I am meek and humble of heart," said our Lord.

Studying the Gospels, we learn. What we learn is that Christ came on earth for the sole purpose of doing His Father's will, which was accomplished by dying for us, His brothers, even though we were the instruments of His death.

So if we are meek and if we proceed according to His will, our work will be somehow connected with the Redemption, and it will certainly involve suffering and that suffering will almost surely come to us through the instrumentality of other men.

The price of belonging to God's family is to have brothers like that.

The proof of belonging to God's family is that we can love them.

4
By the Waters of Babylon

*"Blessed are those who mourn, for they
shall be comforted." (Matt. 5: 5)*

EVEN THE MOST DEVOUT CATHOLIC'S LIFE IS EMPTY
IF HE BECOMES SPIRITUALLY COMPLACENT.

REMEMBER ST. PEGGY OF CHICAGO?
She was a high school senior who looked just like the girls in the Coca-Cola ads who pause for refreshment after school with the captain of the football team and the editor of the school paper. She was like them, too: popular, vivacious, fun-loving, wholesome, well-groomed and modestly dressed. Indeed, Peggy was the personification of the teenage American way of life, and I'm sure her parents could have modeled for those attractive couples pictured in the magazine ads choosing a long-wearing wall-to-wall carpeting, or setting out with their two children on a togetherness vacation in the latest model family car.

But Peggy had a secret, and a secret life. She planned to be a nun. So at parties (in which her life, of course, abounded) she would unobtrusively decline further refreshment after midnight. This was before the relaxation of the Eucharistic fast. And while her schoolmates still slept in the morning, she was quietly off to daily Mass.

You used to be able to read all about Peggy in little pamphlets in the back of the church. I am sure she was invented in a well-meaning effort to dissuade anyone who thought only creeps enter the religious life, but I was always torn between thinking how it must have flattered God to have Peggy choose Him when there were so many attractive alternates, and wondering how anyone who was cross-eyed would dare knock at a convent door.

There are probably lots of Peggys or near-Peggys in our convents. By now they should be principals of grammar schools at least, and they are surely adored by all the pupils. But unless they have had a great awakening, they are not saints. And unless we have a great awakening about our Christian ideals we won't get to be saints either.

The awakening begins with that facet of perfection which is represented in its perfection by the third beatitude: *Blessed are those who mourn, for they shall be comforted.* It has the effect of shattering that nice harmony we have established between the world and God, and then it gives us new eyes for seeing God everywhere, even in the streets of Chicago.

The third beatitude is the operation of a gift of light, the one called Knowledge or Science. Sometimes the Holy Ghost strengthens us, sometimes He warms us, and sometimes He enlightens us, depending on what part of our supernatural organism He is purifying and perfecting. In this case it is faith which is growing stronger and more pure.

All through our natural and supernatural life we need light, because it is by light that Knowledge comes. Knowledge *is* light. Without light our eyes cannot see. Without the light of reason our minds cannot understand. Without the light of faith we cannot believe the truths of Catholicism. Without the light of glory we cannot see God.

Two gifts, Knowledge and Understanding, take away some of the veils which shroud mere faith: Understanding, by way of penetration of the mysteries of God; Knowledge, by bending our souls into an attitude of truth about ourselves and the created world. Understanding is directly related to contemplation, and we are not concerned about it here, while Knowledge makes us judge correctly of the things of this world because we see them as they really are. Sometimes they call Knowledge the science of the saints. Or, again, they say that "the spiritual man judges all things." By faith itself we know more and higher things than are possible to reason, but by this augmentation of faith we see familiar things with new eyes.

How do familiar things look in the light of this gift of Knowledge? They look like dung. "I count all things as dung," St. Paul said, "for the excellent knowledge of Christ."

Nobody wants dung. If a Thunderbird, or a ranch house, or a new dress, or being president of the ladies' sodality looks like something not worth having, who is going to break his heart over it? So the gift of Knowledge is a liberating gift, breaking all those silken cords by which we are held to worldly things. We were trying, oh so painfully, to moderate our love of money, or good food, or our ambitions to excel in the eyes of men — and then, often suddenly, we see the emptiness of it all, our will is free and no longer held by its own desires.

It is a terrible and irrevocable experience, like falling out of love. One day a young man is pinioned to a pair of blue eyes and mincing walk. The next day the pink clouds have disappeared, the mincing walk is only irritating, and as he sadly contemplates his neglected studies, he knows that this particular ensemble of delights can never captivate him again.

Of course it isn't always this suddenly that our dormant gift of Knowledge starts operating. Ordinary-born Catholics like Peggy have to work hard to awaken it, and when they do they experience a kind of second conversion. We'll return to them in a minute. The sudden effects usually accompany adult conversions or result from shattering experiences, especially those in which all your friends desert you and you are held up to public ridicule.

The things of this world just naturally look like dung to people of a melancholic temperament, and while this is not the same thing as the gift of Knowledge, it is analogous to the negative side of the gift. It enables the melancholics to see things in perspective, and even from a natural height they look pretty unattractive, or at least it can be seen that they are unequal to the task of satisfying the human heart. That is why melancholics weep. They are often artistic, and though they are not generally liked, our superficial world greatly admires their profundity.

The trouble is that the modern world doesn't bother to ask if they are profoundly right or profoundly wrong, and many a modern philosopher who is deep, but profoundly mistaken or morally warped, has a baneful experience.

Excellent examples of the gift of Knowledge in operation are to be found in the autobiographies of converts. *Seven Storey Mountain* is remarkable in this respect, but *The Confessions of St. Augustine* is even more so. Both Thomas Merton and St. Augustine (who is the prototype of the melancholic saint) bring out the emptiness of their former lives, although the circumstances of those lives were those the world generally admires. Their worlds were empty and their hearts were restless, and now they weep for the world, for their sins, and for the time they wasted before they knew God.

Peggy, and the ordinary American Catholic, is in a quite different position. These people have always led good lives because they had the help of supernatural grace and the infused virtues. Except as an aid to nature, their faith did not overflow into temporal matters. Add to that the fact that they live in somewhat sheltered circumstances, and you see why they don't have a penetrating judgment of the world. Peggy's uncle is probably an alcoholic, but that can be looked on as a purely personal tragedy. She reads about terrible crimes, but you don't have to be a Catholic to know that there is evil in the world. It is precisely the emptiness of the world that she can't see, because she can't put herself in the place of those who do not know Christ, nor penetrate their hidden spiritual hunger.

That's why the Peggys of America, the good Catholics who frequent our churches, are not apostolic. They are really devout worldlings. Not sinfully worldly, but good-pagan worldly. They lead orderly, temperate, mildly prosperous, neat and conscientious lives, with due regard for God but regulated by reason and governed by prudence.

They are not foolish enough to go on to become saints, nor does the clergy usually encourage them to do so. As a matter of fact, they have reached a kind of dead end in their spiritual efforts. You can only go so far along the route of human order and perfection. Then it is a matter of growing older and richer with the years. Considering the vast numbers of American Catholics like this in our disordered society, it is in a way a wonderful achievement, testimony of the power of the Church. But considering the need for saints and the dearth of apostolicity, not to mention the horizons of supernatural perfection which might be open to them, it is a tragedy.

How should people go on to this sanctity? Should they try to destroy the regularity, discipline and goodness of their lives?

No, of course not. But it will do them no harm to be told that they are in a rut, and that even though they have conquered the excesses, there is still worldliness to be reckoned with. Are they detached from nice clothes, nice furniture, a certain standard of living, security, or even from their favorite rosary or a diet of the better sort of television programs? What have they given up for Lent? Probably cigarettes or candy. It would be much more profitable to shut out the torrent of worldly opinion, considerations and recreations which fill their mental life, for faith is nourished by interior silence, solitude and prayer. Plus some very good spiritual reading according to their tastes.

The great St. Teresa of Avila, though a nun, lived in such a state as theirs until she was about 40. It was when she stopped going to the convent parlor to see her friends that the change came. Meanwhile the effects of her tepid life were most clear in the area of mental prayer, which she had even abandoned completely. People who are interested in worldly things beyond what is necessary to their state, do not like to withdraw into their own souls to find God to talk with Him. Even good Catholics do not like silence. It is understandable that unbelievers, tortured as they are by a sense of sin, must have a radio or a TV set constantly going to prevent their meeting themselves. But why Catholics?

And why do Catholics like to multiply devotions instead of practicing the simplicity of mental prayer? In my experience even members of the nocturnal adoration societies have to be kept "stimulated" with talks and vocal prayers during their hour of adoration. Without the practice of mental prayer, daily Communion will only be a support to a naturally well-ordered life. Charity is materially increased, but is as it were, bound. Further progress in the spiritual life is dependent on a radical change in the top executive. Up until now, we have been in charge and the Holy Ghost has been our servant, supplying supernatural help under our initiative. Things are now ripe for Him to take the reins, and for us to become His instruments.

When the Holy Ghost does start to take the initiative (because we have been docile, and cleared away some of the obstacles and prayed) the transition is marked by the increased light of the gift of Knowledge. This has the effect of lousing up forever that neat little life of ours, which is why we don't have to do it ourselves. Furthermore, it is going to be a long, long time before things get orderly again, so at first it isn't a very welcome gift and lots of people want to scurry back to the solid ground they have left. But they can't go back for one reason or another (which God has brought about: in prayer it is a complete inability to meditate) and they can't go forward because they can't see ahead. The reason they can't see ahead is because they are entering what is known as the dark night of the senses. It is caused by the blinding increase of light in our souls. We are, so to say, being supernaturalized. Sometimes it feels like nothing, and sometimes it hurts. However, even though we can't see the source of the light, or understand what is happening to us, we get a clear view of a lot of things which we missed before, even though they were there. The stars are around all the time but we see them only at night.

It is this superior view of the familiar which characterizes the gift of Knowledge. A thousand people could tell us what it looks like and even if we believe them it isn't the same thing as seeing it ourselves. But it helps, and it can go a long way toward the formation of the Catholic mind in the service of the Church.

We can study even if we are not yet ready to weep, and those who have lights can communicate them to others.

So it would not be out of place to say something about the view of reality given by an enlightened faith.

First of all, Christ who is so ignored by our secular society is really the light of the world, and the light by which we now see: a steady light, from a single source, giving a comprehensive view. By it we see that the world is sitting in darkness and in the shadow of death, and that we are too, insofar as we are worldly. Or rather we were. Though we still live outwardly like Mrs. Jones next door, we have lost our complacency. We know that there is light somewhere and we are going to find it somehow.

We see Mrs. Jones differently too. Formerly we thought she was getting along fine. In fact we were rather ashamed that we couldn't keep up with her in reading good books, gardening, painting and such (the world is so full of a number of things, I'm sure we should all be as happy as kings), because she seemed to have such an appreciation of the good things that God made, even though she never went to church or prayed or talked about religion. Now we see that she is in darkness, that all her hobbies and talents aren't going to get her out of it or save her from the reckoning that comes with death, and that probably quite literally she doesn't know any better. We begin to feel stirrings of apostolicity, a longing to get the Christ-light in us out from under that barrel.

Looking farther afield, we see countless people groping in the darkness, studying it, cursing it or organizing it. Blind leaders of the blind on every hand. We see the marriage counselor solemnly studying in detail the frictions resulting from the mating of an imperfect man with an imperfect woman and hoping to patch things up by tipping her off about what annoys him and vice versa. "Don't you see," we want to shout, "that if they stop that, they will do something else, and that what they need is help from grace to bear with one another to sacrifice and really improve?"

We see a vast army of sociologists measuring and counting and computing and interviewing and fact-finding, and pitifully hoping that if they get more men and more money and make more studies they will find out what the world well knew until yesterday. We see factorylike colleges and universities from coast to coast, where expensive truth-hunts are underway. The first rule of them is: "No fair turning on the light of Christ."

Then we see thousands of psycho-analytical couches where anguished people excavate the deep recesses of their own interior darkness, unsupported against despair by Him Who is our only hope. And then those others who are organizing the darkness, and binding whole peoples in the chains of allegiance to their master-minding Prince.

Everywhere we look we see darkness and death and emptiness and despair and the absence of Christ. So we really see God everywhere, but as spurned or unknown, as a stranger in His own land. That is why we weep. And that is why we feel like strangers too. Like the psalmist, we sit by the waters of our secular Babylon and weep. How can we sing to the Lord in a strange land?

Then we begin to see the stars. First the Church, radiant with light, a beacon of hope shining in the darkness. Then holy people everywhere, binding up wounds, guarding truth, radiating light and love, adoring Christ. We begin to be comforted. We are ashamed to remember that once we hoped all would go well in a worldly way with us, our neighbors and our world, without the Cross and without Christ. It would have been worse not to have felt His absence. It would have been terrible if the Redemption were only on the periphery of the human situation. We begin to see its magnitude, its central position and its radical importance. We begin to see the responsibilities of a Christian. We are comforted by an inner peace which overflows from harmony with reality, and we long to comfort the whole world with the love and light of Christ.

For this is the apostolic beatitude.

5
The Saint, The Crackpot and the Secular Social Reformer

"Blessed are they who hunger and thirst after justice, for they shall be filled." (Matt: 5:6)

SOMETIMES, IT SEEMS, YOU CAN'T TELL THEM APART — AND THEY GET CONFUSED, TOO.

SAINTS ARE OFTEN CONSIDERED CRACKpots. Both look equally foolish to the president of Planned Parenthood Association, the vice-president of the bank, and the ordinary man who is sure which side of his bread has butter on it.

One the other hand, the secular social reformer is often considered a saint on that account. Dag Hammarskjold and Albert Schweitzer are contemporary examples.

What all these three have in common, the saint, the crackpot and the secular social reformer (hereafter referred to as the SSR) is that they are all intent on doing big good things. It would be wonderful if the similarity ended there, as it should, but alas, matters are much clearer and neater on paper than they are in real life. Experience shows that low-grade saints, like most of us who just barely manage to lead a supernatural life, are usually an alloy of sanctity and crackpot, or sanctity and SSR.

This shows up when we begin to practice the fourth beatitude: *Blessed are they who hunger and thirst after justice.* It and the next (Blessed are the merciful…) constitute a plateau of the active life which precedes full development of the contemplative gifts of the Holy Ghost. At the height of sanctity, some several light years further on, when all the gifts of the Holy Ghost operate almost continuously and find no opposition in us, there will come another sort of activity which overflows from full contemplation, and far greater things will be done with ease, perfection and success. The great achievements of the canonized saints, such as the reform of Carmel, the writing of the *Summa* and Francis Xavier's conversions in the Far East belong here. On this present, lower plane we are more like people who have just begun really to love God and are anxious to prove our love by doing heroic deeds and conquering the whole world for Him.

There are a few people, though not so many today, who despise activity. They should be reminded that God Himself is pure act, and that it is by our actions that we do good to our neighbors. Even natural, human activity, which is necessary in every life, is meritorious if we are in a state of grace, and Pope John XXIII has recently announced a plenary indulgence every day for the faithful performance of our ordinary work offered to God.

The activity which characterizes the fourth beatitude is different from our ordinary daily activity in two ways. For one thing it is bigger and harder, and for another we are "passively active," because the initiative and the strength comes from the Holy Ghost, while we are busy consenting, co-operating and trying not to get in His way. Forget about "justice" for the moment and concentrate on the aspect of magnanimity, because it is the gift of fortitude which is at work in this beatitude.

Even on the level of a natural virtue, fortitude is the stuff heroes are made of, but on the level of the gift of fortitude, which perfects the virtue, God supplies us with His own strength and power, first to do things beyond our natural human capacities, then later to do vast and perfect things for the good of the Church, and when necessary (no matter where we stand in spiritual progress) to be martyrs.

It is the first degree we are concerned with here, the things that are too big for us without the gift, and which we are going to do with varying degrees of imperfection because we are imperfect. As a matter of fact, as soon as we stick out our necks we are going to expose our imperfection.

A certain woman I know is engaged in a heroic but depressing apostolate, in which she does much good. As far as feelings go, she hates every minute of it, because it so clearly points up her own faults, inadequacies and weaknesses. She might, she points out, have stayed at home, where living was much more comfortable and where it was easier to be agreeable and helpful. There she was generally regarded as a saint by her family and neighbors, and she began to think she was a saint too, for her virtues had not yet been tried.

The great St. Teresa noted the same painful yet sanctifying effects of the active life: "Since I have been prioress, burdened with many duties and obliged to travel a great deal, I commit very many more faults. And yet, as I struggle generously and spend myself for God alone, I feel that I am getting closer and closer to Him."

The first mark of the fourth beatitude is that we are moved to stick out our necks, and right away we look like crackpots to the worldly prudent, who include some of our nearest and dearest.

"Where is the money going to come from?" is the first question they ask.

"God is a millionaire." (What other answer is there?)

"What if something happens? What if you get sick?"

Here again there is only one answer. "God controls all these things, and I frankly don't know how He is going to manage. Sufficient unto the day...."

Let us consider a common example — the problem of the uneconomically large family. It is normal for married people to have children, difficult for them to avoid procreation without sin, and virtually impossible to support them as one might wish to do. Thus the task of raising a large family in our present economic order is often heroically virtuous.

Well, that's the way it is. We have to be heroes these days, just to lead ordinary lives, and even at that we are lucky we aren't behind the Iron Curtain, where far greater heroism is the daily lot of the Catholic.

Married couples might just as well make up their minds that they are going to aim for sanctity whether they like it or not. They must have a bold confidence in God's power to keep supplying extra loaves of bread, and no matter what their failures, there will be no doubt that they are being schooled in heroic virtue, and that love in that state increases freely.

Of course married people are not the only heroes-by-necessity, even in the United States. There are Negroes, dehumanized factory workers, migrant workers and many others.

Why not, then, reform the social order? Why not make it easier to be good? It is a laudable idea to reform the social order, and it is here that we find the saint-SSR. Unfortunately he has yet to discover, or is perhaps only beginning to discover, that the reform is already in its final stages, only it is not under the auspices of the Holy Ghost.

Its answer to fertility is birth control; to all Negro problems, integration; to mechanized work, more mechanization combined with increased leisure; to unjust material rewards, equality; to irksome authority, rebellion. Under this reform, the overall remedy for state of affairs in which it is difficult to be good, is one in which it is both impossible and unnecessary to be good.

Quite recently, the saint-SSR could be found in a study group at the University of Havana, proclaiming that the Castro Revolution was Christian Humanism.

Now, perhaps, you will find him in an Alabama jail, sitting apart from his fellow freedom riders, and wondering what his sacrifice and hardship and effort has to do with God after all, and if and how it helps the Negro.

Or maybe he is that young man falling asleep in the next pew, who more often than not misses the seven o'clock Mass these days, because he is so busy trying to beat the Communists at their own game. He has mastered parliamentary procedure, he is reading Marx and Engels and Lenin, he outstays the outstayers at union meetings, he organizes against the organizers.

But the Communist Party designedly fills the lives of its rank and file to overflowing with activity, so how is anyone going to keep up with them and lead an intense Christian life too? First our saint-SSR gets bone-tired, then he lets the supernatural supports slip, because it is easier to read Marx than St. Thomas and easier to picket than pray, and then the enemy's cause may begin to look rather reasonable after all. Consider the lamentable case of priest-workers who defected to the Communists in France.

Still another saint-SSR is likely to be a social worker who has just returned to her chic little apartment, lonely and discouraged. At this point she would like nothing better than to get married, and she is asking herself why she had to spend so many years and so much money for professional training to arrive at such a modest and common desire. Has her ambition to help the unfortunate been phony all the way along? Honestly, the results of her efforts are not world-shattering. Worse still, they don't make her happy. Yet she has tried to do the right thing. Perhaps she had more fervor before she took her training, but maybe that was because she was younger. In any case, what can one do without training? Everyone says you must have prestige, and you can't even get a job without a degree.

But we cannot try to solve all the problems of the social apostolate in this article. We are discussing the activity which is the first fruit of the mystical life, and all we need to say is that the neophyte saint stands in great danger if he throws all his energies into the reform of the social order within the secular context, for it is the secular context itself which is the root cause of all our present social disorders.

What is the test for someone who wants to do great things for God and feels called to work toward social reform? How is he to know whether his activity is the work of the fourth beatitude?

Well, his work does not qualify just because he aims at social justice, even if he keeps one eye glued on the papal encyclicals. It's true the beatitude says that those are blessed who hunger and thirst after justice, but Our Lord had higher things in mind. All theologians hold that the justice of the beatitude means holiness, in the sense of the just man the Bible talks about, or the justice that we are to seek first along with the kingdom of heaven. We are not running the same race as the Communists or the Socialists. It is the love of God which is urging us on to demonstrate the love of our neighbor in a practical way, and it is the gift of fortitude which is operating.

So as a rule of thumb, we can compare means and ends. If we are using commensurate natural means to a natural end, then the gift of fortitude is not necessary. We don't need God's omnipotence if we are sufficiently potent ourselves. Strikes, propaganda, freedom riding, demonstrations, picketing, all these are natural means. On the other hand, if a mere nobody, a bookkeeper in some government bureau for instance, converts three people and rectifies two marriages among his co-workers almost without opening his mouth, by sheer force of example and radiating Christ, it is clearly a supernatural work. And at the other extreme is the "activist," who kills himself with work and organization and talk, with virtually nothing to show for it. He has a spiritual malady.

It is the lay apostolate which best exemplifies the exercise of this beatitude in our contemporary society. It has included saint-crackpots who have bitten off more than they can chew, and saint-SSR's who have labored like mountains to bring forth mice. There have been partial successes and partial failures. There have been a few accomplishments, some light spread, some people converted, children in a large family raised somehow.

Yet looking back, one sees something curious. The big product of the lay apostolate has been its by-product. In the midst of follies and failures a new kind of Catholic layman has been formed. For instance, I remember (with humiliation) an early Young Christian Workers' group which set out to restore all things in Christ with an inquiry into the condition of washrooms in New York offices. This isn't quite as silly as it sounds, but almost. The Jocists in Belgium started by cleaning up the factory washrooms, so not knowing where to begin, the YCW group began there, and without really considering that the washrooms in our skyscrapers are among the marvels of the modern world. But it shows how naïve they were about what was rocking society, while at the same time they thought of themselves as the shock troops of a social revolution.

Anyhow, these girls turned out to be marvelous. They were transformed. They were responsible, apostolic and generous. They had a special quality which never has worn off. Similarly, all the apostolic movements left their mark on those who joined, however much or little they otherwise accomplished. The Catholic Worker, the YCW, the Christian Family Movement and the Legion of Mary, all did something for their "graduates" which all the Catholic colleges together couldn't produce.

And isn't this exactly what the beatitude promised?

Nothing whatever is said in it about the success of projects, but only blessed are they who hunger and thirst after justice (read holiness) for they shall be *filled*.

And so it happens, right here in America, and under our very eyes.

6
Enlightened Self-Interest

*"Blessed are the merciful, for they
shall obtain mercy" (Matt. 5: 7)*

HAS ORGANIZED CHARITY PUT AN END TO OUR
OBLIGATION TO PERFORM THE WORKS OF MERCY?

NOW, DON'T GO THINKING OF YOUR-
selves as "angels of mercy," students are advised at the
beginning of their nurses' training. Quite a few spirits
droop when the instructor goes on to paint a glowing picture
of the "professional woman" or "doctor's assistants" they are
about to become. There is no point asking her what she has
against angels of mercy. The secularization of charitable works
has a long history of which she is probably innocently unaware.

There is no point, either, in reviewing that long history. It
will be sufficiently depressing to consider the end result, which
can be summed up this way: Modern methods and techniques
for accomplishing what used to be called the works of mercy
are not channels for the supernatural virtue of charity; they are
straight jackets restraining its exercise.

This central fact has to be carefully considered in connection
with the fifth beatitude: *Blessed are the merciful, for they shall
obtain mercy.* A simple exposition of the traditional teaching
on this subject would be of help to almost no one if it were to
disregard the perversion of traditional channels for the expres-
sion of Christian compassion.

There are 14 so-called works of mercy; seven corporal and
seven spiritual: to feed the hungry, to give drink to the thirsty,
to clothe the naked, to harbor the harborless, to visit the sick, to
ransom the captive, to bury the dead; to instruct the ignorant,
to counsel the doubtful, to admonish sinners, to bear wrongs

patiently, to forgive offenses willingly, to comfort the afflicted, to pray for the living and the dead.

These make up a very special sort of human activity, essentially religious. The nursing instructor to the contrary, these works are not professions. A nurse is not valuable because she knows how to cure diseases; that is the doctor's art. Her special role is solicitous care of sick patients, for which she needs a certain skill and knowledge, greater today than ever, but mostly compassion and love.

The works of mercy are not businesses, either. They are not to be done impersonally and for the sake of the money.

A few years ago the Cardinal Archbishop of New York tangled with the gravediggers in Catholic cemeteries on this score. They went on strike for higher wages and better working conditions. The Cardinal told them in effect that they were impious, that theirs was a work of mercy and that they had no right to strike. They answered that the only difference, then, between a work of mercy and any other work was that you couldn't strike and you were underpaid.

The whole episode made quite a stir among Catholics, with violent defenders on either side. The fact of the matter is that both sides were right and the organization of society is what is wrong.

Burying the dead is a work of mercy; but it is not now organized as such, even in Catholic cemeteries. Gravediggers are not drawn to the work out of piety. They do not have a confraternity, a patron saint, regular spiritual exercises, or set prayers for the dead whom they bury.

They do not wish to live in a spirit of poverty commensurate with their obligations as lay people. They do nothing to hallow their work (at least corporately), nor does the Church. In return the work does nothing to hallow them. But it still remains that digging a grave has more spiritual significance potentiality than digging a trench of about the same depth for sewer pipes.

The main reason it is so difficult to do the works of mercy in a fitting way today is because so many of them have been taken over by a secular government or private secular agencies, which are committed to a policy of ostracizing God and all supernatural spiritual considerations. Parallel services run by the Church are spiritually inhibited in varying degrees by financial and regulatory entanglements with the secularists, as are the religious who usually run them. But it is the lay people who suffer the greatest duress.

A Catholic teacher in a public school cannot instruct her ignorant pupils in religious or moral truth, even if these are the areas of their most desperate need. So what could have been a soul-satisfying and merciful work for dedicated and holy women turns out to be just a job made tedious by the proliferation of paper work (which is part of the mysticism of a secular "profession"). Meanwhile, lay teachers in parochial schools are outsiders, lacking the security, status, respect and spiritual privileges which belong to the nuns. Besides, they are not paid as much as teachers in public schools, even though more than the nuns. The result is that, with notable exceptions, the caliber of lay teachers in parochial schools is below that of Catholic teachers in public schools, which makes it even harder to know where to start a reform.

Except that we do know where to start: we start with ourselves. And this brings us to the fifth beatitude: *Blessed are the merciful, for they shall obtain mercy.*

You will remember that all the beatitudes are grounded in the gifts of the Holy Ghost, each one being an especially perfect act of a particular gift. Which gift for mercy? You would never guess, because right away you would be looking for a gift that makes hearts bleed with compassion, whereas it is an intellectual gift. It's Counsel, the gift which perfects the virtue of prudence.

The gift of Counsel is just what it sounds like; it's the Holy Ghost telling us what is the right thing to do or to say in present, difficult, concrete circumstances. It is a most useful gift for judges, parents, spiritual directors, superiors and people who have to keep secrets without lies.

Do you remember the episode of *Les Miserables* in which Sister Simplice (who had never told a lie in her whole life) was asked by the police inspector if she was alone and if she had seen Jean Valjean? Of course Jean Valjean was right in the room with her, but she looked Inspector Javert straight in the face and said yes, she was alone and no, she hadn't seen him. Victor Hugo so twists our heartstrings that it is difficult not to believe Sister Simplice's remarkable record of honesty was all for the purpose of telling the big "good" lie, and had nothing to do with God. And certainly we get the impression that she has no alternative to lying except to betray his presence. But here is where the Holy Ghost would probably have come to her aid with the gift of Counsel ("probably" because He operates the gifts, we cannot use them as we please), inspiring her to say or do something, which naturally we couldn't think of that quickly or at all, which would not be a lie but would put the Inspector off the trail.

Counsel is really God's prudence. He knows all the hidden factors that we can't estimate, including the future consequences of our decisions. When we act under this gift we are not in complete control of the situation intellectually, but God is. That doesn't mean we shouldn't think about it and go for advice and weigh things, but it does mean that we are going to get help. Maybe it will be a kind of interior nudge. Often a directive passage from Scripture will come to our minds. Maybe we will have a curious conviction that advice given us is or is not good. Counsel not only enlightens us about what to do, but also pushes us to do it. It enables us to "act the truth" and so it works in concert often with the gift of knowledge by which we see the world in a corrected perspective.

Counsel inclines us toward mercy because God inclines toward mercy, and without violating justice. When a mother isn't sure whether at the moment it would be better for Johnny to be punished or admonished and given another chance, Counsel will come to her aid. Parents who are under the habitual influence of this gift will be consistently gentle and firm, like the father of St. Thérèse of Lisieux. Otherwise they will lean toward being too strict or too soft, according to the predisposition of their temperament.

It is good to understand these gifts, but their ordinary workings are not necessarily connected with the beatitudes. Often Counsel has nothing to do with mercy, and even where it does by way of inclination, it is still not quite the beatitude, for in the beatitude the Holy Ghost counsels us about our own lives. He tells us that the way to bring God's mercy down on ourselves is to imitate God by showing mercy to others.

We all need God's mercy because we can't get to a supernatural destiny by natural means, but it always happens that the people who are farthest from God feel this need of mercy the least. Ordinary, just-barely-practicing Catholics think in terms of the sacraments, the handiness of the confessional and the necessity of getting hold of a priest when you are dying. But those who want to be saints and travel the way of perfection in this life see their need for mercy ever more clearly and develop a great longing for union with God in contemplation. As the gift of contemplation is a great mercy which God gives only to the purified, this beatitude is especially a clue telling the would-be saints how to hasten the day of its bestowal.

Keeping these heights in mind, let's descend to the elementary level of sanctity in which most of us find ourselves, and see how we can begin to practice the beatitude. It so happens that married people have a built-in opportunity to get off to a good start. We nearly all have spouses who commit the sort of minor follies which we would never in the world commit, because our shortcomings are of a different sort. This is where we can forgive offenses willingly and with some expectation of a reciprocal forbearance from our spouses. We don't even need the gift of Counsel because we have the Lord's Prayer (forgive us our trespass against us), but we do need a certain degree of detachment from worldliness so that a little wasted money or a display of vulgarity before the Joneses won't make life seem not worth living. This interplay of marital forgiveness is the great alternative to nagging and it is a wonder that some marriage counselors don't get hep [sic] to it. Their way of exposing faults and frailties may relieve a few tensions temporarily, but it doesn't go very far toward making people perfect, whereas forbearance is a good first step.

If the fault is gross, and one sided, then we can start bearing wrongs patiently, which is much harder, as anyone married to an alcoholic knows. I once spent a week (paying guest) with a noble Italian family which had fallen on hard times because papa had gambled their fortune away. This is even less of a joke in Italy than it is here. There were two marriageable and dowryless girls in this family, and the mother, who was desperately trying to keep them all from sinking down a couple of classes, had not spoken to her husband in years. She acted as though he didn't exist. She introduced guests to the person on his left and the person on his right, ignoring him. Vital messages were communicated through the children. After all, why should, and how could, his wife forgive him except by way of earning God's forgiveness for her own sins? I hope she made it.

Now we come to the emergency use of mercy. Don't forget that the Holy Ghost operates His gifts when we are very holy, when we are in a tight spot, and at His own good pleasure. So when we need God's speedy, special and in no way deserved help, not necessarily to get to heaven but maybe to stay out of jail or feed our children *tonight*, we are eligible for emergency mercy, and the way to get it is to practice it.

Christ told us about this in the story of the unjust steward who, when pressed for the payment of his debts and given a few days reprieve, did just what we would do. He put the screws on the people who owed *him* money. It shows how foreign mercy is to human nature, in case we had not noticed it already. We love friends who are not in trouble, we are very quick to loan money to those who can pay it back, and we are easily generous when everything goes well. But our hearts contract the moment *we* are threatened. It's like the banks calling for payment of notes because a drought or a strike threatens the local economy, though of course that is the precise time when notes are hardest to pay.

Christ wants us to know that Old Scrooge, who doesn't care where we get it from but demands payment pronto, is not really ruling heaven and earth. Back of him is God, Who does care where we get it from, and Who can buy up a hundred Old Scrooges, any day.

Some people call this emergency mercy "sowing." (As you sow, so shall you reap — but a hundredfold.) It seems breathtakingly precarious, but it works. The idea is to follow the beatitude literally. Let's say that Old Scrooge demands $500 by Monday at the latest, and we have only $50. Meanwhile, our brother-in-law owes us $300 since last Christmas. We pay him a visit and learn about his present troubles. It seems he is working only part-time now and his wife is in the hospital having another baby.

The thing to do is to take a deep breath and give *him* the $50, along with some words of encouragement. Then go looking for the $500 elsewhere. God will dilate someone else's heart, or we'll find a few bills in the middle of the road, or maybe Old Scrooge will die in his sleep on Sunday night.

When and if we reach a higher level of sanctity, we'll go looking for trouble, and not just take it as it comes. We'll search out lonely old people, the sick, the unemployed, the friendless and those who are about to crack up. We'll have eyes only for misery of the miserable, without reference to whether or not they are getting their just deserts. We'll imitate God, Who makes His sun to shine on the just and the unjust. Is someone cold, or hungry, or thirsty, or naked, or homeless? What else do we need to know about him? Oh, yes, one more thing. He is Christ.

Our Lord told St. Catherine of Sienna about this. It is in other people that you will prove your love for Me, He said. I don't need anything.

That's why we can look upon all suffering people as Christ, even though they don't act at all like Him.

Those who go to work in organized charities will find themselves in a sea of human misery, but will they not hesitate to have their love for Christ measured by the "professional" distance they are obliged, by secular techniques, to put between themselves and their "clients"? If the house is dirty, they are not permitted to clean it, but must arrange for a housekeeper from the welfare department. If the patient is dying they cannot tell him about Christ's redemptive love. Most absurd of all, if an earnest young student brought up without religion wants to know what is the *right* thing to do in order to do it, they are not allowed to tell him the moral law, but must ask him what *he* thinks. Thus the work of mercy known as counseling the doubtful becomes under secularism a refusal to counsel the doubtful.

It is not because welfare work is organized that it is so frustrating, but because of the way it is organized, so that charity is at best irrelevant to its operation and increasingly is inimical to it. It is therefore not surprising to find intense supernatural compassion seeking other outlets.

At a time when the subways of New York were full of signs saying not to give money to beggars, the Catholic Worker established itself in the skid rows of New York and other big cities, setting up Houses of Hospitality for the agonized offscourings of our industrial capitalism.

The red-light district of Dublin was wiped out by the simple, quiet, spiritual and supernaturally oriented work of the Legion of Mary.

Who knows how many chosen souls have simply withdrawn from welfare as a problem, from sociology as a science and from publicity as a means to perform the greatest of all the works of mercy, doing penance and praying for the living and the dead? Theirs will be the highest and quickest reward, the gift of contemplation.

Yet any of us who in any way show mercy because we know we need God's mercy are a world apart from the humanistic pride which is trying to build a new world without God.

7
20/20 Spiritual Vision

*"Blessed are the pure in heart, for
they shall see God" (Matt. 5: 8).*

MOST OF US HAVE TO LIVE IN THE WORLD,
YET KEEP FROM BECOMING WORLDLY.
IT'S NOT EASY; TO DO IT WE MUST HAVE...

BACK IN MY NUNK DAYS (A NUNK IS NEIther a nun nor a monk but wishes he were; in a more general sense a nunk is someone trying to be holy in the world by the methods of getting holy in a monastery), I once decided I wasn't getting anywhere spiritually and that I absolutely was going to start practicing custody of the eyes.

It was a dismal Saturday, overcast and foggy, and for some reason I had to go downtown. When I came out of the subway at 42nd Street and Fifth Avenue, eyes resolutely fixed on the sidewalk, I could tell there was something unusual going on. People were exclaiming to each other and apparently all looking at something. Nevermind, I was bent on being a saint. So I continued on my way, now practicing heroic custody of the eyes, and it wasn't until late that afternoon I learned an airplane had hit the Empire State Building, plowing into an office which contained several of my friends.

So one of the small side effects of that tragedy was that I saw what a first-class prig I was and I never again tried to practice custody of the eyes in the middle of the world.

But the problem still remained. It isn't easy to live in the world without being worldly, and that's why people become monks. It may be a hard life, but it is easier to find God in monasteries, or at least it used to be.

The way I finally figured it out is that God Himself will be our protection, and that the condition of obtaining that special protection is that we are careful to mind our own business and that our own business is also God's business. Then we can walk on the asp and the basilisk, and trample the lion and the dragon underfoot. We will not need to fear the assault of the evil one in the noonday or the plague that walks in the darkness, because His truth will compass us with a shield.

That shield of truth is especially a gift of the Holy Ghost called Understanding, which we have along with the other gifts when we are in a state of grace, and which works right along when necessary but doesn't do its own spectacular work in its plenitude until we reach the sixth beatitude: *Blessed are the pure in heart, for they shall see God.* This gift is both the result of purity in heart and the cause of it. It purifies, deepens and strengthens our faith.

Let me show you what happens when this gift is neglected by good Catholics, and why it is neglected by them. You know the sort of adult Catholic, usually a man, who is apparently very pure (he doesn't curse or commit adultery) but who is rather bored with God. He hates to talk about the truths of the Faith and he slides into the aisle the minute Father disappears through the sacristy door. How can we account for the fact that although he is seemingly pure he isn't even interested in seeing God? Is there something about death or purgatory that is going to cause a radical shift in his interest from the World Series to the Trinity? He will tell you that he has an exceptionally strong faith, and that he is ready to believe anything that Father or Sister says.

The trouble with this good man is that he believes the Faith on authority, as we all have to, but he has never shifted his attention to the content of the Faith as truth. He will never deepen his faith or enable it to shed light on his life and his little world by always looking at Father or trying to remember what Sister said verbatim. He's like a man who has a gift that he cherishes but has never opened. Consequently the gift of Understanding is of virtually no use to him, and consequently also he is stunted both spiritually and intellectually, which is why his enthusiasms remain on the level of games.

Once a Catholic realizes that the mysteries of the Faith can feed our minds even if they cannot be fully understood in this life, he will become much more sincerely devout. He will gaze long and lovingly at the Blessed Sacrament, marveling that God should be hidden beneath the appearance of bread, and feeling that somehow this loving gaze is good for his soul. It is the gift of Understanding at work.

If he will take a little time to pray and while praying will think about the truths of Christianity, he will find a difference in his life. Making money will seem less attractive; practicing virtue more so. One of the effects of the gift of Understanding is to show us quite clearly what God is not and what is not of God.

Our Catholic may never have thought much about his state in life or the kind of work he does, but there will probably come a day when he is no longer content just to mind his own business but want to be about God's business. A purification is going on. He wants there to be nothing in his life which is secular, neutral, or apart from God — as a woman in love wants there to be nothing in her married life which is not somehow shared with or related to her beloved. "Whether you eat or drink or whatever else you do," said St. Paul, "do it all for the honor of God."

Our Catholic may begin to wish he had been a monk. Or he may become a nunk. Or he may hang around the church all the time. All because nobody has shown him how his business and daily life can be God's business, so that he does not have to withdraw in order to find God.

This is how: God is everywhere, because He is the First Cause of everything that exists, and He has to continue holding everything in existence because it is all ultimately made out of nothing. This is God's immensity. It is in this way that God is present in the center of the souls of even sinners and unbelievers.

Spiritual substances *are* where they operate. So when God gives us supernatural grace He becomes present in our souls in a new way because He operates in a new way. Now something analogous takes place in the lay apostolate. God, Who is already everywhere present in the world to keep it going, wills for us, the laity, to make Him present in that same world in a different, supernatural way. Not by preaching, but by being there ourselves and being holy.

Maybe our apostolate will consist of searching out people to help them. Maybe it will consist in correcting errors or preventing untruths or modifying ill effects or in some other way harmonizing the affairs of the world with God's norms. Maybe, however, we are just meant to be there, loving God and doing our job as well as possible, so Christ can be present and perhaps work in hidden ways by this presence.

It doesn't matter. Whatever our mode of action, it happens that the work we do or the neighborhood we live in or the club we join, these all become vehicles for making God present in a new way, and so they are as much God's business as our business (fully His apostolically, fully ours also in the way of human responsibility), and so we are not divided. So we are further purified, because to be pure means to have no admixture of baser elements. We aim to love God with our whole hearts, and strength, and minds and wills, and at this point we are especially concerned to do God's will in everything.

Meanwhile our imaginary Catholic has a wife at home who is at least equally devout and apparently making even greater progress. It's easier for her because her little domain is less contaminated by secularism, she has more time to pray, at least at first, and she is naturally intuitive. The gift of Understanding works by a kind of supernatural intuition, a swift penetration, and it has easily fitted over her own powers. She loves to read books by such people as Mary Reed Newland, Caryll Houselander and Maria Trapp, all highly endowed with the gift of Understanding illuminating domestic and simple everyday affairs.

Special events in the family are celebrated with great liturgical éclat so even the children get to see God everywhere, in the re-enactment of the events in Christ's life and in the trials and vicissitudes of their young lives. They see the providence of God in everything that happens. The Bible is a revelation of the truths they are living. All this is the work of the gift of Understanding, which purifies by its penetration, and then penetrates even deeper and farther. It is fed by prayer; the spirit of prayer always, or as much as possible; solitary mental prayer as much and as regularly as possible.

Then there comes a day when everything turns into darkness; thick, dark, impenetrable darkness. In the monastery where that monk with the cast-down eyes has been seeing God only in His mysteries during prayer, and in the beauties of nature in the monastery garden, the blackout makes his soul seem empty, his vocation useless and faith incredible; but among the laity the desolation of this dark night is partly internal, partly external. God seems not only to have withdrawn from the soul, but also to have withdrawn His help in the temporal affairs, where there is a concatenation of disasters.

This blessing, very much in disguise, is the gift of Understanding full force. The awful darkness is the effect of too much light. It blinds and it burns in one final terrible purification. St. John of the Cross, whose writings are the great consolation and guide for this period, describes the dark night in terms of a fire burning log. First it turns it all black and hideous (this is the worst period, when our Catholic who seems so admirable to everyone and to himself, just about perfect, will have all his hidden faults exposed and brought to the surface, much as the psychological adjustments of adolescence show in acne), until it is entirely heated and penetrated. Then the log, now purified beyond offering any obstacle, is transformed into the fire itself.

So eventually, but usually not soon, our Catholic will emerge purified and quasi-divinized. What has happened is that the gift of Understanding has subjected his highest faculty, his intellect, to God; and now the whole of his being is perfectly subject to God and perfectly united to Him.

The union has taken place in the will: his will with God's Will, through charity, because he now loves God wholly through the subjection of his most resistant part, his mind. Deep, deep in his soul, to which he now can penetrate in prayer, he is aware of a Presence Whom he can "touch," and in "touching," knows. This is contemplation. Penetrating, blinding, delightful, ineffable. The obscurity of faith remains, however, for God is not seen face to face in this life. Those things other than God but related to Him, and to the salvation and apostolate of our Catholic, are seen with perfect clarity.

We may as well run our imaginary Catholic through the entire course. After the terrible purifications are finished he is not going to retire to a monastery. We can assume that his former position in the world has been abandoned or shaken up. Anyhow, he will return in a different role because he is different. Therefore, it becomes important, as it wasn't important before, to have a look at that world to which he is going to return.

We have already seen it as dung in the third beatitude. Now we must realize that it is the Kingdom of the Blind. Even the light of natural understanding is generally lacking among men, who are wandering around in painful confusion. They cannot see causes in their effects, or effects in their causes. They cannot grasp first principles. They cannot see substances under appearances; they cannot see meaning behind events. They cannot see immaterial reality: relations, abstractions (other than mathematical), ideals, values, hierarchies, souls, sins, goodness.

All they can really do is count and correlate and compute and measure. They are hungering for truth but all they can produce in their frantic search for it is mountains of superficial data, which they feed into machines whose brains compare favorably with their own diminished minds. One day they may come to worship these machines. Meanwhile they are busy preparing for any other quantitatively giant project within their qualitatively narrow scope of operation: They are trying to go to the moon.

So our imaginary Catholic now comes among blind men with great love and penetrating light; not as a philosopher who analyzes their errors and to whom they will not listen; not either as a man who sees but dares not wander off course out of a real fear of being blinded himself. He wanders around them freely for he has 20/20 spiritual vision, unimpaired and unimpairable; prepared to show them the truth at the depth where love and light mingle.

We will have to leave him there. Someday he will die, and then he will go quickly to heaven. For he has already been purged.

8
World Without End

*"Blessed are the peacemakers, for they shall
be called children of God" (Matt. 5: 9)*

DOES A WORLD THAT LONGS FOR PEACE
REALLY KNOW WHAT TRUE PEACE IS?

IT IS FITTING THAT A SOCIETY WHICH doesn't know where it came from or where it is going should be full of people who don't know whether they are coming or going, and that these people should take tranquilizers.

For they must have peace and there is no peace without a goal toward which to tend and in which finally to rest. And there is no concord without a common purpose toward which men can work in an orderly way. Secularism is not only the lack of an end in society; it is the denial of society's end. The "open mind" of our colleges is open only to opinion, closed to any truth as truth. We are not like the pagan societies of Greece and Rome in which the wisest men were looking for the truth, because we have already known the light and rejected it. So secularism is a kind of suspended animation, a turbulence and a disequilibrium. But nature abhors a disequilibrium, so ever faster we are hurtling downward toward that suicidal equilibrium that a falling body reaches when it hits bottom.

Ironically, every step of the way is taken for the sake of peace—of the kind that world *can* give, and that people must have if they do not know the true way to peace.

Meanwhile, at the next desk, in the same supermarket line, negotiating at the same United Nations table, or living next door, are the children of God who acknowledge the Prince of Peace and work toward a world without end, and are increasingly peaceful as they rise toward a transcendent equilibrium.

It is by sanctifying grace that men are first put in the way of peace. Charity directs their wills toward God as their last end and gives them an essential peace of soul. It is only a bare minimum for a Christian to be free from mortal sin, but for lack of this freedom the secularist have shaken the pillars of western civilization to rid themselves of the torment of "guilt feelings." It was a long, complicated process, shrouded with scientism and erudition, but the core is the denial that there is such a thing as sin. The word is now put in quotation marks. It is considered that people behave unpleasantly because of traumatic experiences in childhood, or slums. So note that just on this point, although over several generations, the whole basis of society has moved thumpingly downward. It is no longer on a moral basis. Education and child-rearing were revised in accordance with the new determinism. Laws are gradually being brought into line.

But neither the forgiveness of sin nor the denial of sin does away with temptation, and so the Christian must go to war with his concupiscence or lose his minimum peace, while his secular counterpart has no alternative but to surrender.

Let's take the Christian first. His special temptation may be avarice or lust or sloth or anger, it doesn't matter. Whatever it is, he is not fighting it alone. He has the Church as an external help and the grace which the Church dispenses as an internal help. These are the immediate agents of God's great comprehensive plan for the universe, which is called Holy Wisdom. He can't see this plan very well yet, but he knows that God made the world (the beginning of the operation of the plan), and he can see the Church as God's instrument. He may not even know that the Holy Ghost dwells in his soul to sanctify him, and that this is done through seven gifts, the highest of which is Wisdom. This gift of Wisdom is a participation in Holy Wisdom and so it orders all the other gifts too, starting with the Fear of God, which will help our Christian in a special way not to look for his satisfactions in the things of the world.

While the Christian is fighting with his lower nature, our

secular example (who may be nominally Christian or a diluted or distorted sort) is allowing himself to be convinced that indulgence rather than repression is the answer to his cravings. All this happens gradually of course, a little at a time as the Christian heritage disappears, and is eloquently rationalized by learned men. Avarice, for instance, is defended as free enterprise, certain to enrich the state as well as the entrepreneur, and plain stealing is at the same time severely repressed. The countermovement which this provokes in the name of justice is not entirely comprised of men who are poor in spirit, so the spirit of avarice, now aided by envy, keeps worsening affairs to the point where the economy seeks a new equilibrium on a lower plane of public control.

So it is with all the appetites. Chastity insufficiently defended gives way to a double standard of sexual morality quietly countenanced, then to divorce, then to multiple marriage, then promiscuity among adolescents, then to the regularized sexual sin of steady dating and finally to a sentimental tolerance of unwed mothers. Meanwhile the family has been destroyed, and there is no longer an equivalent substitute, so the situation merely breeds new kind of delinquency.

Let us return to our Christian, who should by now have been guided by the gift of Wisdom to a new level of peace. Reasonably well in control of his own house he now wants to do works of justice and mercy to soothe the world's turbulence.

He will find that the very framework of justice has practically disappeared. Instead of reciprocal rights and duties operating under law with a reinforcement of moral suasion, he will find a general leveling going on. It will even be represented to him that social and material equality is identical with justice, and anyhow machines have largely obliterated the special talents, abilities and skills formerly required by a functional society. The dignity and humanity of men is diminished. They no longer have the intolerable insecurity of dependence on capricious kindness and fluctuating markets, but they have paid a terrible price for their "peace."

Whenever our Christian mentions his zealous desires for serving God he is encouraged to work for social justice. It is explained to him that after all we have a secular society and the supernatural aspects of our religion cannot be brought to bear on it, but all men are bound by the natural law and social justice is not the prerogative of Catholics. So he tries, but he finds he is always moving backward. Instead of action there is a tendency to form a committee. The committee in turn does not discuss the best method of action or talk about principles. It sets up a subcommittee of investigation or fact-finding. He begins to think that even if the work is necessary he is not necessary to it.

Still, there is this matter of the natural law which is even more strikingly violated on the personal level, with birth control, abortion and the threat of euthanasia. No one is interested in his arguments from reason because they see these violations of the natural law as necessary in the higher context of human happiness. He has no answer for them on the level they are supposed to stand.

Then he begins to see the magnitude of the drive for peace on the level of human relations. A lot of the talk he thought was for settling things was really an end in itself, a forum for airing grievances and wearing down antagonisms, comparable to the relief that comes from simply talking about one's evil deeds.

Technology is everywhere glorified because it is so neutral, so purposeless in itself. All men everywhere can be united in praise of literacy. Any government which is popularly elected is thereby blessed, and voting, for whatever party, or however ignorantly, is civic virtue. Consent is the basis of concord and the justification of action. Contraceptive information can be given if husband and wife ask for it, murder is mercy-killing if the person wants to die. Social workers' methods cannot be questioned because they use them only on people who come to them for help.

Surely by now he has thought of joining a neighborhood study group, because modern problems are very complex and perhaps ignorance is his trouble. Fortunately one is just starting in his town, to discuss Great Books or some facet of foreign policy, run by a man who has been specially trained in this sort of thing. The leader turns out to be very self-effacing. Apparently he has no special competence in the subject but knows just enough to start the ball rolling. After a while it becomes evident that he has a special competence of another sort, for manipulating groups. He always finds comments interesting rather than true. He seems especially concerned that everyone say something, however empty the brain behind the remark. So much the better if members can get into a heated argument. What is he getting at? Certainly not agreement on the level of truth (although this was what the members thought they were assembling for). But not concord on the level of opinion either. And not social harmony, because he seems happy to destroy the little politeness by which people ordinarily get along.

It turns out that in varying degrees, all the little groups which have become popular from one of our coasts to the other, are intent on defrictionalizing humanity by reducing peoples' reactions with each other to a horrendous new low level. Corporations pay to have their executives go to three and four-hour sessions of sitting around in a circle, unobtrusively goaded by the trained leader into a kind of name calling and faultfinding which would be shocking even if they were all drunk. They will certainly all go back to the plant with greatly diminished dignity and self-respect, even if all hatred is spent. The formula for concord is: provide abrasive situations for rough edges to rub each other off. How far we have fallen from the mutual charity which is the basis of concord in God's plan of Holy Wisdom!

Everywhere, then, our man fails to find a toe hold for saving the world from its own folly. He would be discouraged, except that the gift of Wisdom is urging him on. It intimates that he is not yet ready to do great and good work, that he doesn't know enough, that the answer is to be found in God, who is the All.

So Wisdom leads him to seek God in prayer, and there in the darkness of Understanding he sees that the absence of God is the cause of all the world's pain.

Now Wisdom pours forth her own light in greater abundance and he sees that peace is truly the tranquility of order, the simplification of a multiplicity by a common end. That end is in God, and is God, Who made all things and to Whom all things return by a marvelous harmony beyond our comprehension. He sees that because there is this plan of Holy Wisdom we do not have to worry about fitting into the new order of nothingness here below. For Holy Wisdom govern even this, and there is absolutely nothing, including the holocaust of nuclear war if it should come, which is allowed by God except for the sake of a greater good.

"All things are well, all manner of things are well." In these words or similar words the great contemplative saints have told us what they see when the Holy Ghost has completed His work of transforming them into children of God, when the gift of Wisdom has given them the highest glimpse possible in this life of the plan of Holy Wisdom. From then on nothing disturbs them, or can disturb them, and for so long as they remain in this life they radiate peace.

There had been first that seed of peace, when they received sanctifying grace and so began to cooperate with Holy Wisdom.

This was fortified by their conquest of concupiscence, during which they contributed to the world's peace in a negative way by withdrawing from the rat race for material goods and satisfactions.

Then there was that long period during which they were a disturbing element to worldly concord because they refused to betray the designs of Holy Wisdom in order to keep a job or get a degree or win a promotion or placate a family. They thought their suffering during this period was a kind of martyrdom, but it was really a purification, preparing their souls for the great and transforming peace of union with God.

Now they are ready to do the perfect works of the apostolate. What will they be?

For all their sanctity they still do not know where they will be sent or how God will again rescue the children of men. They can only pray: "Lord, make me an instrument of Thy peace!"

For only God is Wise.

9
Pie in the Sky

> "Blessed are they who suffer persecution
> for justice' sake, for theirs is the
> kingdom of heaven." (Matt. 5:10)

AS THE DAY MAY NOT BE DISTANT WHEN those who put us to death will think they are doing humanity a favor, the last of the beatitudes is of more than academic interest to our generation. It tells us that we should rejoice and be glad if we suffer persecution for our religion, because we will be in the best tradition of the prophets and our reward will be very great in heaven.

At the beginning of this series of articles, it was pointed out that holiness is the work of the Holy Ghost in our souls. This holiness is much more than simple natural goodness. It is even higher than the kind of virtue we practice with the help of the Holy Ghost, and with one eye on our supernatural destiny.

This holiness is qualitatively different. It is the Holy Ghost acting in us, as He sees fit, and with all the resources of the divinity. We act too, but secondarily — consenting, rejoicing, continuously acknowledging that we could never do it on our own, and giving thanks.

Those who reach the heights of sanctity on this earth are almost continuously subject to this divine action of the Holy Ghost in their souls. In those of us who are not yet saints and are far from perfect, but trying, the Holy Ghost takes over only occasionally, when we are especially fervent, or in an emergency.

Yet during that moment, or that emergency, we live on a very high supernatural plane. It may happen in prayer, or in a financial crisis where we show great trust in God, or in a heroic act of forgiveness or pity. We are saints, then, for the moment.

The trouble is we can't keep it up, and gradually our imperfectly mortified appetites, our attachments and our pride, begin to reassert themselves, as the plane of our daily living returns to somewhere near the normal-mediocre.

The one exception to this deflationary process is martyrdom. There we can die while in a state of inflated heroism which would not survive a commuted sentence, and in so dying we go speedily to heaven.

However, it isn't easy to be a martyr, even if the enemies of God oblige us with persecution, so we must study the conditions. One way is to examine the beatitudes more closely.

This last is not like the other beatitudes, synchronized with a particular gift of the Holy Ghost. There are only seven gifts, and this is the eight beatitude. Yet it would at first seem to be entirely understandable in terms of the gift of Fortitude, which underlies the beatitude about hungering and thirsting for justice. Indeed it is the supreme act of the gift of Fortitude, but it is much more than that. Courage is not all that makes the martyr, or we would be hard to explain false martyrdom.

The merit of true martyrdom comes from the virtue of charity, of which it is the supreme act. Charity is the basis and end of all the gifts, and higher than any of them. We can give our bodies to be burned and it won't do us any good if we don't have charity. On the other hand, if our charity is so great that we are ready to be torn apart by African savages or shot in the back of the head in the Soviet Embassy basement for the love of God, then we can count on the Holy Ghost not only for courage but also for counsel so that we will know where to take our stand and how to answer our accusers. For the gifts grow together with charity, and if we are given the grace to love supremely a high degree of the gifts will also be available to us.

Even in the natural order much love compensates for many short-comings. Romantic love makes marital sacrifices easy. Love of a field of learning makes the study of it a pleasure. Love of one's work compensates for a low salary and long hours, and a loving mother will do more for her children than one with greater talents and proficiency but less love. And it is true of the natural as well as of the supernatural order that no man has a greater love of his friend than he who lays down his life in proof of it. It is not to be wondered then, that martyrdom is the short cut to heaven; and it is good to realize this, because we may get a chance to take the short, quick road. However, it is a sobering thought that in the great age of persecution of the early Church, the second and third centuries, the number of apostates seems to have been about equal to the number of martyrdoms.

Persecution, then, also offers a quick way of getting to hell. Yet at that time the sheep are certainly not going to be divided from the goats along arbitrary lines, with the Adamses to the Johnsons going up, and the rest of the alphabet going down; or with every second man saved if he wears a green cap. How then? What can we do about it in advance?

The best preparation, of course, is to be very holy. It will then be normal to have the help of the Holy Ghost, and martyrdom will be welcome. Bishop Ignatius of Antioch, who wanted to be ground up by the wild beasts into the bread of Christ; Polycarp, who begged his followers not to intercede for him with the officials and prevent his death; Cyprian, Bishop of Carthage, who felt obliged to duck one persecution for the sake of his flock, but was able to take advantage of the next; these and all the very great martyrs have gone to their deaths rejoicing, because they were already saints.

They clung to no earthly possessions; they harbored no worldly ambitions. In fact, they were dead to the world and totally detached, and their passions had long since been conquered. They were totally confident in their Faith, but meek as the Lamb of God. They had been purified and strengthened in good works; they had been raised to the heights of prayer. They had been transformed into Christ and possessed Him in their souls. All that remained was to imitate Him in the supreme act of His Passion. To live was already Christ; to die would be only to gain Heaven.

It is all very edifying to read about, but since most of us aren't saints it is not very helpful by way of example. We simply are not thirsting to be beaten and jeered at by our neighbors, or to be calumniated by our fellow workers or even hanged from the corner lamp post. So let's bypass those who did it the hard way, for whom the martyr's crown only capped a victory already as good as won, and see what we can learn about our peers.

In the early persecutions in the Roman Empire there were vast numbers of Christians put to death, possibly upward of half a million, which was proportionately far greater than even the number indicates, because populations were much smaller then and Christians were in the minority.

Although on the books it was against the law for about 250 years even to be a Christian, the persecutions were intermittent. Yet, as the intervals between them lengthened, their fury increased. At the beginning Christians were not hunted out but were put to death only as they came to official notice. Or sometimes the official concern was only for Christian leaders, or the heat was on in one part of the Empire and not another. Toward the end, however, whole populations were forced to adore the Roman gods or perish.

So there came a time when no one escaped the trial, even catechumens who were under instruction. Obviously the vast majority of martyrs were ordinary Christians, lay people in all (but mostly humble) walks of life. Not many of them could have been in the advanced stages of prayer, and they were not segregated from the life of the world. Why did some die gloriously, and others apostatize?

Let's see if we can find out from the nature of martyrdom itself. We have seen that it is the supreme act of the gift of Fortitude. Was the failure of the apostates then a failure of courage? It usually seemed so on the surface. They couldn't go through with it because they were afraid.

However, this explanation does not stand up. There were all kinds of people among the martyrs: old men and young girls, the naturally strong and the naturally weak, the timid and the brave. It would obviously be absurd to train for martyrdom with physical fitness courses or by crossing busy city streets in the middle of the block. Besides, we know that we will have to depend on the gift of Fortitude which taps God's own strength, and won't be given, if it is given, until it is needed.

This is very clearly illustrated in the case of an early woman martyr. She was near the term of her pregnancy when arrested, and so her death was postponed until after the child was born. When she cried out in childbirth the guards taunted her, asking how she could hope to endure the torments awaiting her in the arena if she couldn't stand the birth pangs. She answered that now she was suffering on her own, but then she would be suffering for her Lord and so Christ Himself would support her.

So physical weakness and natural timidity are not obstacles to martyrdom, and it even seems as though moral weakness do not offer an absolute impediment to the action of the Holy Ghost.

Graham Greene has presented the case for the martyr with moral weakness in the *Power and the Glory*. His story of the hunted Mexican priest has a plot almost as nicely contrived as a textbook explanation of the qualifying circumstances for martyrdom. The hero is an unworthy, not a model priest, weak all around but especially in the direction of whisky; yet he has not apostatized. Nor does he provoke his own martyrdom. That's against the rules. The alternatives of death or freedom are exquisitely drawn, and the hinge on the duties of his priesthood. Matters are rarely so clear-cut and obvious in the lay life, and indeed Graham Greene is not nearly so successful with the moral dilemmas of the laity in his other works. The priest is afraid, but he makes the right choice and goes to his death without either protest or exaltation.

Interestingly enough, Graham Greene shows us that his whisky priest could only have saved his soul through martyrdom. In his brief moment of freedom the tentacles of avarice and dreams of luxury had engulfed him, and the reader is horrified, for these are obviously much more deadly than drink.

And that's exactly the way it is; worldliness, not weakness, is the mother of apostasy. The gift of Fortitude can easily supply for a want of courage, but charity is impossible if the heart is divided. The love of God is not like any other love. It cannot be shared. It can overflow on other things and cause us to love them more than we would naturally, but we must first love God with our whole hearts. If we cannot love God perfectly because our own nature is still unruly, that does not matter, so long as we love God as much as we can now.

But what is fatal is to try to love God and Mammon, because that means trying to put other things on par with God, which is already to deny Him His due. The problem is not in the things of the world but in the spirit of the world. It's hard for us to see what is happening, but it is really a war between two spirits; one is the Holy Spirit, and the other is the spirit of the world which tempts us to love it for its own sake or as an end in itself.

This is very interesting. Or perhaps terrifying is a better word. For secularism is precisely this spirit of the world in its purest form, unadulterated by any lesser idolatries. And secularism is the air we breathe.

It is the religion of our public schools and of the air waves. It is the guiding principle of our libraries and our national magazines. It is a major ingredient of all our social reforms and our patriotism; the disease of our art and music. It is the cause of all our hidden hungers and the reason for the failures of our loves and hopes. It is the dead weight of similitude with communism, which paralyzes our national will so that we cannot rise to smite the militant and subversive vanguard of its total conquest.

Sometimes it tells us that God does not exist and that this is the only world. Sometimes it tells us that religion, for those who like it, is a minor facet of life, irrelevant even to the making of a good world. And having long told us that one religion was as good as another, it is now busy pressing the rights of irreligion.

What we must realize is that the persecution is already in its last stages, even here in America where no blood has been shed. For the world does not want to kill us, it wants to convert us. It wants us to be apostates, not in order to put us in hell, because it doesn't believe in hell; but because we get in the way of its plans, we are a sore thumb.

For all that, the devil is probably behind this and we should realize what his intentions are in our regard. We should see that even our neighbors can easily grow to hate us, whether over parochial schools or contraception, or the changing of this law or that.

And they are being egged on by much more sinister forces and much more subtle ones. We can expect every defect to be exploited, every defector to be flattered, every traitor to be rewarded, every advantage to be pressed, every truth to be distorted, every compromise to be urged, every low appetite to be fed.

Much will be done by the equivocal use of words. What does Brotherhood mean? Or Freedom? Or Democracy? Or Peace? Were we wise to consent to refer to our "pluralistic" society? Does this simply mean that there are lots of different religions in America? Or does it mean (will they use it to mean?) that we are happy to have it that way and would not wish it otherwise ever?

If worse comes to worse, there are slanderous rumors to be spread, antagonisms between clergy and laity to be encouraged, or between the laity-of-the-right and the laity-of-the-left, and hopefully a schismatic Church to be established and somewhere along the line there is Church property to be confiscated and special disabilities to be placed upon Catholics.

Death, exile, imprisonment and torture come only at the very end. They are the world's last resort. But the decisive trial of many of us will take place long before then; when we lose our jobs for taking a moral stand, or compromise and keep it; when we start practicing contraception rather then lose our house in the suburbs; when we expose ourselves to false teaching in college out of curiosity or to get ahead in the world.

Many of the Christians in the Roman Empire quietly busied themselves during the penal period in apologetical efforts. They studied their Faith and tried to explain away misconceptions, even though this had little immediate effect. But what sustained them chiefly was the prayer life of the Church, whether they prayed privately at different hours of the day, as was their custom, or gathered for Mass in houses, churches or the catacombs.

When the blood persecutions came, especially if there had been a long interval since the last one, the Church was purified rather than destroyed. For the lukewarm were sloughed off and those who suffered but lived were strengthened. The pagans, already struck by the steadfast conduct of the martyrs, were more and more impressed by the moral purity of the daily lives of the body of Catholics. When it finally became legal to be a Christian at the Edict of Milan, practically the whole Empire had been converted.

As for the martyrs themselves, it was only in the sight of the unwise that they had seemed to die. They had long been enjoying their pie in the sky.

10

The Poor in Spirit

THE BEATITUDES ARE A SUMMARY OF THE way Christians should live — a Summa of Christian living, the theologians say. That's the most important thing to know about them.

The first one, "Blessed are the poor in spirit, for theirs is the kingdom of heaven," was the first of eight set forth by Our Lord Himself at the beginning of the Sermon on the Mount, in which He explained the New Law that He came to establish.

Because the beatitudes are the New Law, they stand in striking contrast to the Old Law. In the Ten Commandments we are told: Don't do this, Don't do that, and we know that if we do we'll go to hell, for they state the minimum requirements for staying in God's good graces.

With the beatitudes it's different. Blessed are these, and Blessed are those, we are told: happy, fortunate and praiseworthy. Why? Because supernatural rewards stream down on them in one way or another. Even here they live in a kind of anticipated heaven.

So the beatitudes are the plenitude of the spiritual life, the measure of the true and full Christian. But whereas the Ten Commandments make sense — even a pagan would realize that murder and stealing are wrong — there is something very foolish about the beatitudes. Consider how for the most part they contradict our own best judgment:

> *Blessed are the poor in spirit, for theirs is the kingdom of heaven.*
> *Blessed are the meek, for they shall possess the earth.*
> *Blessed are they who mourn, for they shall be comforted.*

> *Blessed are they who hunger and thirst for justice, for they shall be satisfied.*
> *Blessed are the merciful, for they shall obtain mercy.*
> *Blessed are the pure of heart, for they shall see God.*
> *Blessed are the peacemakers, for they shall be called the children of God.*
> *Blessed are they who suffer persecution for Justice's sake for theirs is the kingdom of heaven.*

For several hundred years the world has been living on its own best judgment, or rationalism. That's the fundamental reason for the troubles of our time.

The fundamental remedy, then, is to start living according to the foolishness of God, which is greater than the wisdom of men. This is to enter into the mysteries of God, which we do through the practice of the beatitudes and the gifts of the Holy Ghost.

Both St. Thomas and St. Augustine say the beatitudes are, theologically speaking, high and perfect acts of the gifts, each beatitude linked especially with a particular one of the seven gifts, and the final beatitude with them all. Poverty of spirit, as we shall see, finds its link in the gift of fear of the Lord and its fulfillment in the gift of wisdom.

POVERTY OF SPIRIT

Poverty of spirit is the anti-worldliness beatitude. It calls eventually for total detachment of the heart from everything interior and exterior which is apart from God, but it is chiefly concerned with detachment from material possessions and worldly honors.

The trick, in all ages and all conditions of life, is to find some way of using the things of this world (for use them we must; we are not angels) without falling in love with them, so that we may keep our hearts free for the love of God. There never is anything new about the basic problem. If there is a new angle in its solution, it must be because of the novel circumstances in which the problem is set.

Over the centuries it has been found that the quickest route to poverty of spirit is poverty. Poverty voluntarily chosen; not poverty unwillingly suffered. Our Lord Himself recommended this course to the Rich Young Man. "If thou wouldst be perfect, go sell all thou hast, and give to the poor, and come follow Me."

Envy the Religious?

Most religious orders practice a modification of absolute poverty in corporate ownership and security. This enables the religious to carry on their works of mercy, or to devote themselves to contemplation without material worries. It also sometimes takes the edge off the heroism of their abandonment to God's providential care.

Rich people have a habit of bestowing their tax-heavy estates on religious orders. So it sometimes happens that Sisters who eat off tin plates with their food all squashed together, because that's what the rule calls for, afterwards go for a walk in their expensively terraced flower gardens. Priests who wear hand-me-down clothes from deceased members of their orders sometimes have solid gold spigots on their washbowls. Yet they are only making do with what's been given them in alms, and those who do not make do often find themselves paying outrageous prices for what were the cheapest and coarsest articles and materials when the rule specified their use, but are now rare and costly, or must be specially commissioned.

All this is their problem and not ours, but it is getting so that when Mary Jane down the street announces she is going into the convent the neighbors no longer marvel at her as a heroine of renunciation — "Imagine, giving up all that! Such a hard life!" — but they are likely to tell her mother it must be a comfort to know that at least Mary Jane will always be taken care of.

When the laity start envying the religious their material lot, and sometimes it comes quite close to that, things must be pretty tough in the world; And if things are pretty tough in the world we may find we do have a set of novel circumstances which allow for an unusual approach to the problem of poverty of spirit.

Lay Life an Obstacle?

For it has always been thought that the lay life was in itself a natural obstacle to any noteworthy practice of poverty of spirit. "Use the things of this world as though you used them not," laymen are told. It is recognized that a large part of our lives is necessarily concerned with material things, which will almost certainly distract us from the things of the spirit when they don't prove an active temptation. Therefore it is generally thought that the best we can hope for is a well-ordered use of material things consistent with our state in life, a generous disposal of our excess goods, and however much spirituality it is possible to cultivate within this prudent framework. No fireball displays of Christian folly, but lots of solid virtue and much accomplishment in the way of the world's work.

If, then, things are changing in our own time, if a heroic level of virtue is now possible to the laity in general, it must be due to special circumstances which now prevail, and we must learn how to take advantage of them.

The situation can be summed up in this way: a heroic level of virtue is now *possible* to the laity in general because a heroic level of virtue is now *necessary* for the laity in general. Or, as a recent Pope put it: it is no longer possible to be mediocre.

OUR CONCUPISCENT SOCIETY

Ordinarily it is by the virtue of temperance that we moderate our appetites for the things of this world.

There is first of all the natural virtue of temperance which is developed through repeated acts of self-restraint. It keeps our sense desires from exceeding the bounds of reason, measured by need. A lot of labor is involved in acquiring this virtue (more for some than for others), yet its aim is modest: eating habits consistent with health, material possessions suited to one's state in life, pleasures without overindulgence, sex within marriage and without sin.

The normal resistance to the acquisition of this virtue comes from our own fallen nature. This fundamental weakness is magnified by the conditions of our present-day society.

Mixed-Up World

There is first of all simply a lack of order, almost a chaos. There is no firm pattern within which to grow and live. Parents are bewildered about how to bring up their children, or so preoccupied by the instability of their marriages that they exercise almost no discipline. And the home gets almost no help from society in general because we have long suffered a powerful intellectual attack on the whole idea of the cultivation of virtue. Behind many popular theories of psychology, teaching, child rearing and even criminology is the philosophy that human nature is naturally good, not fallen. The will does not have to be trained to resist the lower appetites. Goodness has been redefined as positive or socially acceptable conduct.

As a consequence of this weakness, doubt and denial, there is little of the natural virtue of temperance practiced, whether among Catholics or non-Catholics. More and more adults are at the mercy of their unruly appetites. Even those who do exercise self-restraint often vitiate their efforts because they are misers, health cranks, or power hungry. With Catholics the tendency is to bypass the natural for the supernatural virtue of temperance.

This supernatural virtue of temperance is infused, which means it costs us nothing in the way of effort to acquire it. With it we have an intrinsic facility for moderating our appetites in accordance with a new norm of rectified reason, and for doing more than is required for the practice of natural virtue, fasting for instance. But if the natural virtue isn't there too, underneath, this intrinsic facility in the will cannot easily subordinate our sense desires.

As a consequence many Catholics have supernatural temperance without having natural temperance, though they could easily acquire the latter with the help of the former if they tried. They are immoderate smokers, for instance. They can't cut down. They give up smoking for Lent (supernatural motive), and on Easter they start in immoderately again. They can fast, but they can't diet, or even give up eating between meals.

So it comes about that Catholics are frequently as vulnerable as non-Catholics or modern pagans, to the special temptations of our time against the virtue of temperance. As these temptations have probably never been so great or so widespread, it is now exceptionally difficult to lead a temperate life in the world, even with the ordinary help of grace.

Tomorrow's Necessities

For here in America we live in a Concupiscent Society. It has been called an Affluent Society, from which we can congratulate ourselves that we have licked poverty, crusade-like. But actually, what we have licked is the spirit of poverty. We boast that today's luxuries are tomorrow's necessities, and it is true. Things we never dreamed of wanting, much less owning, are part of every household. They are not there as luxuries, either. Whatever it was we used before or did with our time formerly, is no longer available or possible. Our whole way of life keeps changing.

There are no stockings but nylons, no model-T Fords, no durable, rough, poor people's clothes-though there are some chic and oddly designed rough clothes for fashionable lounging and not for poor people. No one builds big, sturdy, roomy, modestly priced one-family houses with yards any more, but there are plenty of three-room apartments with dish-washing machines, and there are those miniature ranch houses with picture windows.

It's hard to believe that electric toothbrushes will replace the primitive hand-operated kind, or that large numbers of people will buy landsites in the Bahamas, but the fact that these things can be seriously dangled in front of a mass audience shows to what fantastic lengths we have gone.

Can't Slow It Down

It is not so much that we in this Concupiscent Society are all panting after material possessions, though we are; it is that the system runs on our panting. We've worked out a system of production that keeps turning out too many things and can't be slowed down or the whole economy will fall apart. So the only way to keep from a bust is to work on the consumers, continually increasing their already voracious appetites. A massive assemblage of brains is at work on this, mostly in the advertising business.

"It's our job," one of them said, for they are often very frank, *"to make people buy what they don't want, don't need and can't afford."*

"What they don't want." That means that our unruly desires, bad as they are, aren't themselves doing the stimulating. Most of the talent of the nation is preying on them, and maybe a few dark principalities and powers as well. We may as well have a good look at what we are up against.

"What they don't need." Remember that need is the rational mean of the virtue of temperance. And this indicates the direct attack that is continually made on our efforts at moderation. It's odd how little we are aware of this. One reason is that the day of reckoning has not yet come. A spoiled child will be agreeable as long as you keep ahead of his demands. It is only on the day he is first refused something that we see what awful harm has been done. Yet there are little warnings all along. If it really hurts when the supermarket is out of the aquamarine Kleenex that just matches the bathroom, we are pretty badly hooked.

Another reason we don't realize that our appetites are far in excess of our needs is that needs are no longer related to function. A file clerk now needs to dress like a contestant in a fashion contest, not because this in any way relates to filing, but so she can maintain her status with the other girls, the approval of the men in the office, and fluid relations with the personnel people. On a deeper level it is so she won't see how empty and unsubstantial her life has become, but she is usually unconscious of this. Inflated and artificial needs prevail everywhere. And they keep rising. This is not entirely the fault of the advertisers, but they are certainly alert to exploit the opportunities.

Finally there is that last consideration.

"And what they can't afford" It isn't enough for us to be divested of our substance; we must also become indentured to some bank or loan company. This started long ago with installment buying, merchants making it possible for us to use major purchases before they were fully paid for. A temptation to extravagance perhaps, but it now looks like the very pinnacle of frugality in a world of mushrooming credit cards and lots of other fancy invitations to enjoy now and pay later. Most of these are strictly usurious schemes for homing in on the big spending.

Why Resist?

Who can resist all this? And why resist? Isn't this the way all people live now? Doesn't my very job depend on making a good appearance? Isn't it right to give my children these advantages? And most tellingly, there is no other way to live. Reason has no other mean to judge by. There are no more states in life, there is only status.

Oh yes, there is a mean: the budget. It's not functional, but it's concrete. A man ought to live within his income. But since we have been buying things we can't afford for so long, and mortgaging our salaries to do it, not a few of us are poised on the brink of financial ruin.

If it takes our minds off God and the things of the spirit to dream of the perfection of our material existence, this is nothing compared to the solicitude we now have to exercise. (Be not solicitous... remember?) We wake up in the night to worry about unpaid bills. They give us ulcers. We can't retrench because everything is part of the pattern, and besides we've already used the things we bought, even though we're still paying for them. And these are usually just the things on which we should retrench.

So we have to count every penny that goes out for really necessary things like food, and a lot of our time is spent trying to figure out if the large economy-size jar at 67 cents is really a better buy than the two-and-a-third ounce jar at two for 43 cents.

"You can't serve God and Mammon." But we find we are serving Mammon, and it is a very painful servitude indeed.

If at this point someone comes along and suggests we practice poverty of spirit, we may be tempted to throw the checkbook at him. The very mention of poverty will send us scurrying back to another futile effort with the bills and the budget, from which we are likely to emerge thinking there's nothing for it but to go to night school and study for a better paying job. Hardly a step in the direction of detachment.

A better approach is through fear.

FEAR AS A FULCRUM

Most of us do not have an overwhelming appreciation for the supernatural life in our souls (we don't find our highest pleasure in prayer, for instance), but at the same time we fear to lose it. Not because we love it so much, but because the consequences would be so dire.

This is curiously parallel to our situation in the world. We are not in love with our jobs either, and when the bills pileup we would even be willing to part with our high standard of living it we could step gently down to one slightly more modest. But somehow or other we have to buy it whole and the alternative is ruin. So we are afraid to let go.

It certainly seems as though the devil is behind this whole modern situation and that he has led us down the garden path, quietly burning our bridges behind us. He is careful not to force any choices until he wears down our spiritual sensibilities as much as possible. That's what worldliness does, wears down spiritual sensibilities. Then he brings us to a point where simple choices turn into all-or-nothing decisions. It doesn't matter which side the choice comes from. Maybe having another child will ruin a whole way of life, and not having another child will involve mortal sin.

Maybe a man is asked to do something shameful in connection with his job, or maybe he is tempted to do something shameful on his own in order to hold it; a little lying or stealing; some shady juggling of accounts.

Whichever way, the stakes are high. Anyone who reads the papers can see how often men make the wrong choice out of worldly fear. It is especially sad to read about prominent Catholics who are jailed for bribery or falsifying accounts or perjuring themselves, all because they cared more for keeping their children in good schools and their names in the papers, flatteringly, than for right relations with God in their souls. Perhaps their big mistake was to make the fatal choice on their own without appealing to God for the special help that would have been theirs.

This special help would have been an increase of filial fear through the help of the Holy Ghost. Then it would have been a battle between the fear of material ruin, with all the circumstances stacked up by the devil, and the supernatural loving fear of God which is based on trusting love and dependence on Him as a father.

Same Kind of Struggle

This is the sort of struggle St. Augustine went through in the garden, although in his case it was over chastity. It is the same lack of temperance which is involved in sex and in worldliness. It was a terrible spiritual battle that St. Augustine fought, and not without seemingly miraculous help from God. As he had not yet been baptized, he did not have the gifts of the Holy Ghost as we do. Anyhow, he wept and he prayed. Every time he considered giving up the lusts of the flesh he saw that it was impossible. But he was finally face to face with the certitude of Christianity and his very soul would have been destroyed if he now refused to accede to the truth he so clearly saw.

Augustine finally saw that the way out is up. "Grant what Thou dost ask," he prayed, "and ask what You will."

We say it a different way: that God never asks the impossible. We are never asked to choose ruin, we are asked only to choose God. This is rather like throwing ourselves on His mercy. For love of Him, and fear to lose His friendship, we rise to a new relationship of vital filial dependence.

The more there is at stake in such a crisis of conscience, the higher the holiness which will result from its favorable issue. In St. Augustine's case, he knew that in choosing God he would be choosing Him totally, perhaps because that is the sort of man he was. He knew he was choosing celibacy. As it happened, he remained celibate, and chaste, all his life, but always because of God's grace. The temptations remained, to remind him of his continued dependence.

Our problem here is worldliness, but the effects are the same. In choosing God we are likely to be throwing ourselves on His special Providence, and this is a good thing because we can't for one minute forget whose hand we are eating out of. It doesn't seem like an ideal way to live if you are a married man with a family. It would be very imprudent for anyone to choose to live this way on his own. But we are here supposing that it is the only possible way for a Christian to live, at least for the moment.

And God can provide, of course. He is the first cause of everything that happens in the universe. He can either bypass the secondary causes, as in miracles, or He can move them, warming hearts, eliciting generosity, putting ideas in people's minds.

Childlike Dependence

God actually wants us to become as little children, wholly dependent on Him. But that doesn't mean He wants us to live hand-to-mouth forever. He's not opposed to the regularized poverty of the religious life, or the virtue of temperance, or even budgets and regular incomes.

However, we can be sure that God does not like having whole nations full of people so intent on what they will eat and wear, or so busy storing grain in their barns, that they can hardly spare a half-hour on Sunday to pay Him lip service. We can be sure also that God is not pleased as we become more and more beholden to worldly gods for our daily food. And especially that He is not pleased with the cockiness of men who think they don't need God any more, that they can run the universe by themselves.

So whenever some little family gets behind the eight ball in our Concupiscent Society, God may regard them as escapees from Mammon, to be entered into His service, and not just to be sent back behind the nylon and dacron curtain after a few lessons in making ends meet. In a word, He may wish them to become saints, to help along the plan of His Wisdom.

FEAR — BEGINNING OF WISDOM

Wisdom, we know, is God's over-all supernatural plan for the universe. It is not just the part we can understand with our reason, like the natural law; it includes everything. But because it includes everything, like the distribution of God's graces, and whom He is going to make a saint and how He is going to bring good out of evil, and hidden things, and secret things, and future contingent things, it is shrouded in mysteries.

Now as long as we run our lives only by reason and plan everything ourselves and insist on seeing where we are going, we participate in the plan of wisdom at a low level. But if we can make some sort of total submission to God, if we can surrender the autonomy of our lives to God's special direction, then we enter into the mysteries, where we are divinized and God does great things through us.

It is the gift of Fear of the Lord which raises us to the supernatural plane of the plan of Wisdom. This is the level of the operation of the gifts, starting with Fear and ending with Wisdom. It is obvious why this is so; we are in a situation of total dependence on the special help of God.

Here we come to an important difference between the laity and the religious. A monk who is living on the level of the gifts has already arrived at a high degree of detachment, interior as well as exterior. He not only has a sense of total dependence on God as his father, but a high degree of poverty of spirit.

Life Preserver

Lay people who have an emergency infusion of filial fear in difficult circumstances are like passengers who have just dumped all their worldly goods overboard (or seen them washed over by the waves) in a storm, and are terribly thankful to be alive. Nothing seems valuable to them by comparison, but by tomorrow they may be regretting their loss.

Therefore, while we should be careful not to despise the emergency action of the gifts in our soul, even if it doesn't last, we should see that in these times it may well be in the plan of God's wisdom for it to last, if we cooperate.

The test is really whether or not we develop poverty of spirit before we get settled in a situation where we can relax a little. And at this level you don't become poor in spirit by thinking about the things you are going to give up, but by concentrating so hard on something else, which is higher and better, that the attachments fall by the wayside without even being noticed.

As a matter of fact, the something else has to be the plan of God's wisdom and that particular part of it He has reserved for us.

To begin with we don't know what that is. We can suppose that it has to do with the apostolate, but all we can know for sure is that it is God's hidden will, and we can pray for that.

It is not a bad idea to remember how God led the Jews through the desert to the promised land. They had been uprooted from the Egyptian servitude, harsh but alleviated by the flesh-pots. All the time they were in passage, and had no means of supporting themselves, God fed them manna. It took 40 years because they went around in circles. They could have got there much faster it they had been obedient. When they finally arrived, they were given the means to take care of themselves, but they were given the sacred duty of carrying out their very special part in the plan of God's wisdom.

A Cause to Champion

Today God's special people are those who are in the Mystical Body. And in a way Christians are cut loose today from a temporal order which is failing. Even if they are not in financial difficulties or jobless, they are bored and unsatisfied. They want to enlist in the cause of Christ and most of them don't know where to throw their energies or how—even when they are not captivated by the spirit of the world. It is only within the higher plan of wisdom that they will find where they belong. They have to leave the fleshpots of Egypt for the desert, where they will be sustained by some sort of manna, while God leads them to their special functional place in the Mystical Body.

They may not even change their home or their job, in which case it will be largely a spiritual and interior transformation that will be effected. Or they may go to Vietnam, or to the other end of the social scale—down or up. But there will be some sort of desert and some sort of manna, until we forget about the fleshpots of Egypt and are ready for God's service.

HOW MUCH IS ENOUGH?

We should by now begin to see that it is within the lay apostolate, broadly conceived, that we are going to find the norms for deciding how we should live, materially speaking. Instead of a "state in life" in the natural, temporal order, we must find our functional places in the lay apostolate and the Mystical Body. Then we will see not only how much we really need, or how little; we will be able to practice temperance within these new limits, because we will already have acquired poverty of spirit in the process of being guided by God our Father to whatever work He wants us to do. Not only that, but we will have His continued help in supplying those needs if the temporal means are not sufficient.

Don't think of these functional positions in the Mystical Body as religious jobs. For the most part we will continue in the work for which we have been trained, but do apostolic work either within or without them. If we find that the job pays much more than we need, now that we have our concupiscence suppressed, then we will be giving away money where formerly we were having difficulty making ends meet. There won't be any difficulty about a large family, if that's what God wants us to have.

To the degree that we have acquired poverty of spirit, we will want to be poor and it may be that there will be many people who will have the apostolate of becoming poor, as a sort of testimony. Certainly many who have jobs that don't matter will find other jobs which do matter even if this means a considerable loss of salary.

It may happen, it often does happen in what is called the "full-time apostolate" that a person will lead a very insecure life, almost without possessions except for a change of clothes, and yet use, and even enjoy in a disinterested way, some of the great splendors of a technological and wealthy society — things like luxury airplanes, world travel, luxury accommodations at hotels. It is as though God can trust them because they are working for Him. But He won't trust them too much. He sent St. Paul a goad to buffet him and keep him humble.

THE REWARDS

All the rewards of the beatitudes are in the supernatural order, but we don't have to wait until we get to heaven to enjoy them. All the way to heaven is heaven, but this truth doesn't hit us over the head as long as we are mediocre Catholics. When we get to the level of the gifts and the beatitudes, we really begin to experience it, and that is why the reward of poverty of spirit is the kingdom of heaven. It really means that we have made the giant step, we are no longer prisoners of the earth but have our treasure in heaven and so our whole orientation.

The special mark of poverty of spirit is joy. The worldly have pleasures, which are on the whole depressing; the poor in spirit have joy. This joy is bound up with the freedom which comes with poverty of spirit.

There is a special dividend which comes with poverty of spirit in addition to the freedom and the joy. It is a wonderful new appreciation for material things. Now that we have learned to despise them for God's sake, and we have shed all our possessiveness and cupidity, we can cherish and admire them as God's.

No Short Cut

There is no short cut here. We can't start appreciating before we are detached. Besides, we have too many things, and there must first be a process of simplification of life.

We always think of St. Francis when we think of appreciation and of poverty of spirit, because he was the great poor man of all time. But he sang the praises of nature, the sun and stars, and birds and beasts. This is not going to be a natural manifestation for most of us, and besides there is much to be done close at hand.

Above all, we need to stop seeing everything in terms of money value. Everything has a price tag, as they say. When we buy a car we are already thinking of selling it (what is its trade-in value?). We think of houses as good or bad investments. And college educations, even high-school educations, only as leading to high-paid jobs. People collect pictures and furniture and even friends, with an eye on profit. And we think money will buy everything from love to world peace.

It's almost as though the whole world and its beauty was hidden under a coat of filthy lucre and false glamour. Only poverty of spirit can discover the beauty hidden deep down and can separate it from all the ugly accretions and purify it by offering it to God.

THE SACRED FLAME

There is a beautiful old legend which shows symbolically how a man can become poor in spirit by guarding the divine life within him.

It is about a crusader named Raniero di Raniero, a worldly, proud and cruel man, whose wife left him because he was destroying her love. That's why he joined the Crusades, where he fought so well that after Jerusalem was taken, with much needless bloodshed and pillage, he was allowed to be first to light his candle at the tomb of Christ.

Quite inadvertently he comes to vow that he will bring his candle flame, unextinguished, back to Our Lady's altar in the cathedral of his native Florence and that he will make the journey alone.

He has hardly set out before he realizes he has to ride backwards on his horse to protect the flame. Because of this he is taken by robbers who take his horse and armor, but give him an old nag instead.

So it is as a poor man and an apparent madman that he makes his journey. With every almost-failure, his longing to succeed increases. With each new adventure he changes, learning things to which he was so blind in the days of his arrogance. He comes to appreciate the most simple things, and common, peaceable people. He comes to realize why his wife left him, and why he could never win her back with feats of daring. His preoccupation with the flame becomes almost an obsession.

As he nears Florence he remembers the trophies he left in Jerusalem and the new conquests and honors that could be his, but all these thoughts give him no pleasure. Then he realizes for the first time that he is no longer the same man who set out from the Holy City.

"Verily this flame has re-created me," he thinks. "I believe it has made a new man of me."

So, gaunt and ragged, still riding backwards on his nag, and never taking his eyes off the flame, he enters his native city. At first nobody recognizes him and he is mocked as a madman. Then they do recognize him and refuse to credit his story.

In the end, of course, he lights the altar candles, and afterwards settles down to live happily and temperately ever after with his wife.

11
The Meek

ON CURSORY ANALYSIS, THERE DOESN'T seem to be anything we need less in our time than meekness.

For one thing, to press meekness upon people would seem to be urging them back into a servitude from which they are emerging for the first time in history. Women, children, underdeveloped nations, workers, depressed groups, black men, all the people who are by nature or circumstance normally weak, are now beginning to have their rights recognized and look forward to an appropriate share of the good life. They have rebelled in the name of justice; what has meekness to offer them?

On the other hand there are many people who are, so to say, too meek. They put up with personal situations which give them ulcers or nervous breakdowns. They tolerate pornography and various sorts of corruption. They surrender their freedom for the sake of security.

Clearly then, on the surface of it there is no Christian teaching so inappropriate for our times as meekness. We need to stress what is positive and strong in Christ's teachings and soft-pedal meekness as much as possible.

Central Virtue

Unfortunately this is not possible. Nothing is so characteristic of Christianity, so central to it, as meekness. Our Lord Himself said that we were to learn of Him on account of His being meek and humble of heart. He said the meek were blessed, and that they would inherit the earth. Furthermore, Our Lord's example is predominantly one of meekness and its accompanying traits: kindness, gentleness, consideration, respect, returning good for evil, walking yet another mile, and blessing those who cursed Him.

If, therefore, meekness has no present-day role, then neither does Christianity; the enemies of the Church are right in urging irreligion.

Yet those who fear meekness have truth on their side too. When they say that meekness is impossibly difficult to practice or that it invites various sorts of disaster, they speak from experience of reality.

However paradoxical it may seem, what is needed is not less meekness, but more. It is not meekness which has failed, men who have failed to practice it. But by so doing they have so worsened conditions as to make it necessary for us to practice meekness in a heroic degree. It remains the one remedy.

Today a small motel will fail on the same spot in which a giant one will immediately prosper. An especially gifted singer or baseball player will be ferreted out of the most obscure corner and made world-famous overnight; while a middling talent will go begging even in his own town. A new soap, or a new color of an old soap, or a high school or a TV program takes a million dollars to launch and is in full business the next day. Everything has to start big to succeed at all.

Correspondingly, it is also impossible to be spiritually mediocre. We ought ideally to be able to work up to holiness step by step; first doing what we can on our own, then harder things with the help of grace, and finally letting God take over to do in us what is totally beyond us. But if the lower rungs of the ladder are broken we have to find some way of getting directly to the top or we perish. But God's help will not be denied us in the measure we need it.

Think of our problem as having to take a giant step over a canyon. Anything less than a giant step and we topple in; one great stride and we are safe on the other side.

So it is for most us in the case of meekness. Let those who can start at the beginning. Let the others not be discouraged, for not only is it possible to start higher, but the higher degrees comprehend the lower, at least virtually, so having the higher they may also acquire the lower and consolidate their gains. A lovely voice can do anything a middling voice can do, better and easier. Of course a lovely voice is a gift — but then so is heroic meekness.

A Matter of Docility

Meekness is best defined in terms of docility to the order of reality. Sooner or later this docility involves the suffering of injustice, but that is accidental, not essential to meekness, even if it is the most striking of its effects. Meekness will remain in heaven where there is no suffering.

We can distinguish three degrees of meekness, according to three different orders of reality, or truth.

1. The docility of the irascible passions of the soul to the direction of reason.
2. The docility of the individual person to the order of society and the world ordained by God.
3. The docility of the Christian to the order of revelation and the mysteries of God's Wisdom.

Only the third and heroic degree of meekness is that of the beatitude and the meekness of Christ.

We shall here begin with the lowest.

Meekness as Self-Possession

Meekness in the first degree is a moral virtue annexed to temperance. Its function is to subject our irascible passions, especially the passion of anger with its accompanying irritation and impatience, to the control of right reason.

Anger is good but, as everyone knows from experience, it tends to be excessive and can easily become so vehement as to overwhelm reason. The virtue of meekness, which is built up by repeated acts of self-restraint, diminishes the passion of anger so reason can never have a chance to direct it.

Uncontrolled anger has terrible consequences for society. It is the cause of dissensions, quarrels and wars. As these contentions are usually about material possessions and worldly honors, meekness depends heavily on poverty of spirit. But no matter how it starts, anger tends to breed more anger in a chain of resentments.

When Mr. Upperdog's wife wakes up cross, she proceeds to ruin her husband's day at the breakfast table. So he arrives at the office in a temper and barks at his assistant, who, not daring to bark back, harbors resentment all day until he can unload it on his wife for being late with the dinner. Mad as a wet hen, she blasts the children, who leave in tears and are presently heard quarreling with each other.

If any one of the people on this chain had "absorbed" the unjust anger with meekness, the process would have been instantly halted. We don't ordinarily appreciate our debt to the meek who quietly quench the fire of anger by letting it spend itself on them. We think they are doormats, that they lack personality. But they know what they are doing and it is a real act of charity. Mrs. Calvin Coolidge who was a very retiring first lady, said she thought her greatest service to the nation was to let her husband blow off stream to her after it was generated by unjust criticism in the press.

Prelude to Madness

If the bad-tempered are the enemies of social peace they are even more their own worst enemies. So terrible is their wrath, as they turn white or red, become deadly silent or shout, that everyone is afraid of them. Rightly so, for their vengeance can be terrible. It is hard on this account to regard them as spiritual cripples, but that is what they are. Since they cannot learn how to walk as men, they are hopelessly unable to turn the race of life. They ruin all their plans when they are half under way. They lose their friends, jobs, opportunities, and of course their peace.

It is not without significance that mental hospitals used to be madhouses, their inmates madmen and some of their corridors, violent wards. The terminology has been softened, but the basic situation remains the same, which is why the drug that has brought about a symptomatic relief is fittingly called a tranquilizer. By it fires raging out of all control are extinguished. The tranquilizer of the soul, the spiritual tranquilizer, is meekness.

The ideal time to acquire the virtue of meekness is, of course, in childhood, the earlier the better. This is the only time when the causes of anger are trivial compared with the problem of anger itself, although this may not seem so to the child.

However it is the exceptional child today who gets anywhere nearly adequate training in moral virtue and does in fact learn self-discipline. Some of the most conscientious parents have been persuaded that knowledge is the all-important thing and that the will doesn't need training. Vast numbers of other parents are themselves inadequate, negligent, preoccupied with their own marital difficulties or busy working. When they are around they often spoil the children by way of compensation, and also by way of making it doubly difficult later for them to learn self-control.

Even with spoiling, and almost certainly with quarreling, children grow in years (but don't mature) carrying a burden of deep resentments toward their parents and perhaps toward all authority. This is the anger of frustration which not seldom drives teenagers to acts of real violence, touched off by some apparently trivial incident.

Nature cannot safely be thwarted; it always kicks back. Children need training in virtue as a plant needs water and sun. But once they have adult problems to cope with they can no longer make a simple beginning.

However, we are here concerned not with the training of children but with the spiritual life of adults in face of the reality of their present conditions.

There is no point in saying, "Isn't it a pity that Mary was so poorly brought up," as though the damage were irreparable.

It is still more useless to urge Mary to count to ten when her pent-up hostilities threaten to overwhelm her. That's far too little and too late.

Shall we then offer the now almost universal therapeutic advice? Shall we tell Mary to see a psychiatrist? That depends on whether or not her case has progressed beyond the spiritual realm into that of mental illness. If it has, a psychiatrist might help. In all cases short of madness, however, the basic remedy is a higher degree of meekness, where reason can be strengthened and in turn strengthen the will.

The second degree of meekness has a quite different emphasis from the first. It takes us out of the realm of effort into that of understanding, of justice.

The Rebel and the Robot

The second degree of meekness is docility to the real order of the external world. It involves the subordination of man to man within a complex and organic social whole. It has a close affinity to obedience, or duty.

The meek man here is the one who sees the order of the world and accepts his own place in it. There he sinks roots, grows, develops and perfects himself. He is not concerned whether the circumstances of his life are humble or exalted, pleasant or unpleasant, difficult or easy, but only whether or not they are meant for him.

This meekness has its basis in the truth that man is naturally a social animal and that society is an organic whole composed of all manner of subordinate, functional wholes. Individual man does not stand nakedly alone but is heir to the experience and wisdom of mankind through tradition; he is nourished by a myriad of ties and institutions through which he also expresses himself.

We are born into this complexity of relations, which is not only an enrichment but a limitation. By them and our native abilities our future path is roughly marked out at birth. We are specified by a definite sex, a certain culture, a degree of health, a national homeland, a certain temperament and appearance, the possession of such and such gifts.

Not a Rebel

The meek man, then, is first of all the man who accepts "his lot"; not fatalistically but realistically. He is willing to grow according to his own potentialities and to sink his roots deep into the ground in which he has been planted. He is neither rebellious against the role in life assigned him, nor covetous of those more favored. If he is a boy he doesn't wish he were a girl. He doesn't regret he is an American, or feel that he was born in the wrong century. He isn't ashamed of his parents. He does not despise his own appearance or harbor the sort of ambitions by which men try to soar above their proper place, by concentrating on making money for its own sake and the status it can buy.

Indeed, the meek man is grateful for everything he is and has. He sees himself as owing on every side debts which he can never repay. He has an awed respect and reverence for his parents who gave him the gift of life, and then spent themselves for him in a lifetime of work, hardship and sacrifice. For his country he feels a patriotism much like the reverent gratitude he has for his parents, knowing that he could scarcely exist without the peace, culture, protection and other advantages which stem from ordered communal living. He is loyal, devoted and law-abiding.

This second degree of meekness, this effort to repay in gratitude, reverence, respect and obedience debts which can never be strictly repaid, is known by the general name of piety. It is an effort to be just in matters which exceed the ordinary measurements of justice. It is a natural virtue which gains strength and perfection from infused supernatural help. It spreads out from family and country to all the other associations and subordinations in their proper degree.

The meek man is aware that his teachers' concern to form his mind and pass on a heritage of learning deserves his honor, obedience and conscientious study. He defers to all old people as the visible representatives of the forefathers on whose shoulders he stands; to all women in honor of the woman who gave him birth. Even toward equals and chance acquaintances the meek man is markedly polite and kind, out of an almost instinctive respect for human nature itself and a sense of responsibility to the common good.

Obviously the first and second kinds of meekness are meant to grow together, with reason as the bridge between the internal order and the external. As the passions are brought under the control of reason by the will using repeated acts of self restraint, the reason itself is rectified, becomes "right reason" with respect to the people and circumstances of life.

Sinking Roots

As a person matures, meekness becomes less a matter of accepting the circumstances of birth and nature which he can not escape anyhow, and more and more a free choice of fitting circumstances. He has to sink roots of his own, and meekness helps him sink the right roots in the right place. The meek man does not have to seek out the one girl in the whole world with whom he could be happy, but a suitable girl; and if he does not have his appetites and passions under control, he is likely to make an unfortunate choice which will jeopardize his whole future happiness.

Next to an unhappy marriage, there is no more poignant source of human misery than to choose the wrong life work. A man's wasted talents never cease to torment him, while the job that he does fill is never filled with joy or ease. No matter how humble a work is, it should always have the aspect of a vocation. A work to which a man is "called" by the outside need and natural inclination, and to which he responds through meekness.

Within a suitable marriage and a fitting career, all the lesser manifestations of meekness can flower. There will be a respect which accompanies subordination, a deference which tempers authority, a gentleness toward friends, neighbors and acquaintances even a respect for the materials and tools of work, for the requirements of a job well done

Centering on God

Above all, of course, the meek man will center his acceptance of the order of the work and his place in it, on God Who created it and created him and determined the essential circumstances of his life; to whom therefore he owes constant worship and obedience.

Without God as its base, the whole structure collapses, because it is no longer possible to root the basic circumstances of life in necessity. Every obedience, deference, rule and authority rests on another and higher one in a chain of dependencies which all collapse in a heap if they do not lead back to a beginning which is solid and independent.

If all authority does not ultimately come from God, it is all arbitrary and can only maintain itself by compulsion.

But since the social order is always imperfect because of sin, meekness involves not only humility but suffering. That is why it is usually defined in terms of *suffering* injustice and *forgoing* vengeance. It enables wives to put up patiently with bad-tempered and unfaithful husbands, as St. Monica did; it helps children to obey imperfect parents, citizens to endure bad rulers and slaves to obey harsh masters.

Throughout the ages people usually have had no choice but to suffer the injustices accompanying subordination; the only question was whether they would sweeten the inevitable with the virtue of meekness or kick against the goad. Yet a free society is only possible in the measure that people are willingly subordinate.

Today we think that a free society is possible only if all men are equal and don't have to be meek. This is an aberration, an aberration we have because men have destroyed the legal and traditional sanctions which reinforced the order of society.

Problem of Belonging

The penalty of rebellion in today's world is a terrible new suffering: man's exile from his own world. This world was made for him, but it is no longer under his control. The earth is his home, but he is nowhere at home in it.

I once attended a session for the review of cases up for dismissal in a mental hospital. A lovely and very earnest German woman was brought before the social workers and psychiatrists. It seems that life with her husband was so difficult that she had cracked under it, and the question arose as to whether or not she should now return home. She wanted to know, and she begged to be told, whether she *ought* to go back to her husband. It would be difficult, she said, but if it were the *right thing to do*, she could bear up under it. Only she had to be sure. In other words, she was prepared to be meek, but she wasn't prepared to be a fool. It wasn't suffering she dreaded, but useless and meaningless suffering.

No one would tell her it was the right thing to do, or even that it wasn't. The staff sat in clinical righteousness, asking the poor woman what *she* thought about it and how she felt, as though the whole matter rested on the weakness of her so recently shattered emotions.

But she was appealing for the strength of the "ought," the law outside herself which would have made her will strong to be meek. Without it, her choice was only between a useless hospital existence and a shameful servility.

Eventually she would choose the servility, with all its bleak prospects, as simply the lesser of two evils. For the same ignoble reason many of us end up settling for the dull job, the nagging wife, the pointless college courses, the endless succession of tests and questionnaires, and our own mediocrity. Not with a meekness of conviction, but with servility, because we can't stand the agony of not belonging.

The problem behind all problems of our age is this problem of belonging. It is the central political problem, the major economic problem, the chief concern of sociology, the great religious problem. Above all, it is the more or less acute private torment of almost everyone. It is the theme of many a modern novel, the battle cry of the angry young men, the key to the nihilism and absurdity in modern philosophies and arts.

Those who have destroyed the order of belonging are the rebels; those who settle for security at any price are the robots.

Even those of us who may not personally have wanted to enter the arena are caught in the ruins of inhuman reconstructions: we are all of us part rebel, a lot robot.

Modern-Day Rebels

It will be useful to have a look at the rebels we still see about us. Here is a partial list of some of the most familiar:

Individualists, who deny the social nature of man.
Atheists, who deny the existence of God.
Divorcees, who deny the indissolubility of marriage.
Truants, who refuse to be educated.
Juvenile delinquents, who resist parents and policemen.
Feminists, who refuse the role of women.
Skeptics, who deny the possibility of knowing truth.
Positivists, phenomenologists and kindred philosophers, who refuse to consider other than sense knowledge.
Anarchists, who won't be governed at all.
Egalitarians, who war against subordination as such.
Freethinkers, who make their own morality.
Beatniks, who resign from the order of society in contempt of convention.

These recall to our minds some of the ways in which Western civilization has been razed, in which treasures of truth, discipline and order have been exhausted. Rebels are like prodigal sons, who have spent their inheritance and ours. The frolic of spending continues, but the rebels are tired and the pain of not belonging has become unbearable.

They, and the millions who are rootless, alienated, alone, afraid, outsiders, disinherited, lost in an absurd world, strangers and exiles, are now willing to settle for slavery and servitude.

No longer able to endure the ever-open mind, they are prey to any demagogue; sick of being on their own, they look for a leader, any leader; afraid of unemployment and being propertyless, they hunger for the guaranteed security of a large impersonal industry or government bureaucracy; weary of skepticism, they long for commitment of any sort.

Actually, the strait jacket of our new society has been building for along time, because the revolt was based on a denial of a "given order." God as the root of necessity and the source of authority was the first to be denied. From that time men have speculated about the different and better order they could figure out themselves, and they have used every opportunity to experiment with their ideas. Only recently has the resistance of the old order finally crumbled.

On Being "Sold"

It is this man-made order then, which has us in shackles. It works entirely from the outside and by compulsion, though the compulsion is often cleverly veiled. It is the manipulation of the hidden persuaders, the propaganda continuously pouring over communications channels, the oratory and flashing personalities of politicians.

We are not being "sold" by a dispassionate presentation of truth, in arguments aimed at our intellects. Nobody is trying to build up our virtue so we can fit into the new order as free men. The effort is always the other way around, with its aim to destroy our will to resist.

The new order is like a vast machine of which we are machine parts. Our free will counts for nothing, because we have only trivial decisions to make; our skill counts for nothing, because machines have replaced crafts. Our brains count for nothing because we are allowed only a superficial cleverness within the presuppositions of the system. It does not even matter whether we are good or bad, because virtue is not relevant. Indeed, moral license is encouraged as an outlet for vitality not needed on the job. Moral license gives the masses an illusion of freedom while binding them with double chains.

How can meekness be an instrument of belonging in such a concentration camp? A man has all he can do to hold to his very humanity by resisting some of the pressures. Increased docility would be the suicide of the soul. This is the world of the robots, in which diminished men become faceless units.

Still Doesn't Belong

Paradoxically, although the robot has sacrificed his freedom for the sake of security of belonging and being taken care of, although he has even put his soul in jeopardy, he still doesn't belong.

For to belong means to occupy *your own place*, and in the world of robots everyone is expendable and interchangeable. To this end even the family is being destroyed, by divorce and working mothers here; by communes and state nurseries elsewhere. Men count only as units in a mass, as members of a group able to be manipulated by their passions or by the threat of withholding food.

Of course things are not yet so bad here in America, yet everyone has the feeling of being forced into a mold which diminishes him, whether it is a house that is luxurious but too small for the growth of a family, or a job which is not made to anyone's measure.

So the problem of belonging remains. The second degree of meekness can tell us all about it, can show us why we hurt where we hurt, can point up our dilemma, but cannot help us to belong in a world where the structure of belonging is in such disrepair.

The only answer is a superior degree of meekness, based on the higher reality of the world of Christian revelation, and it is to this that we now turn.

The Lamb

The third and highest degree of meekness is based on the new relationship to God, the new framework of belonging, which Christ won for us. This is our adopted sonship by which, as St. Paul says, the Holy Ghost moves us to cry "Abba, Father."

How different this meekness is from the other two kinds is best known in an analogy.

Previous to our redemption we had been living in a house where there were a lot of rules about the proper place for everything and the hours we were to keep and how we were to conduct ourselves and what relationships we were to have with the other tenants, especially on the matter of who was to boss whom. All these rules were made by the owner of the house, whom we never saw and whom we could never approach for special privileges, or release from one obligation or another. The house rules were inexorable. If you didn't get down to breakfast, you went hungry. If your subordinates didn't obey, you had to use force.

The owner's goodness was everywhere evident. Tenancy was rent-free (at least as far as *he* was concerned, though there were extortionist fellow tenants on all sides); the ground was beautiful (except for tenant litter); the system was admirable (or would have been if people kept the rules). Those who were grateful, obedient and meek, who *kept* the rules, made out better in the long run than those who tried to improve their own lot in disregard of the rules and at the expense of others. Nevertheless, it was impossible to escape a measure of suffering and a good deal of bleakness.

Marvelous Intervention

Things might have gone from bad to worse, but the owner chose to intervene in a marvelous way. Instead of descending in wrath to mete out punishment and reinforce the rules, he outdid himself in goodness and sent his only son to pay everyone's debts, spread forgiveness and make it known that the owner offered everyone, good and bad alike, adoption as his sons and heirs.

We are not forced into this new relationship, but if we consent to join the family, so to speak, we will know the liberty of sons. Instead of being subject to impersonal rules and fated circumstances, we will be under the personal, loving care and guidance of a father, who may have special plans for us and who is ready to put all his wealth and power and knowledge at our disposal when we need it.

The old rules and order of precedence will remain, at least for the most part, but they will diminish greatly in importance. The Father is not bound by his own rules. He may choose to love a son who, as a tenant, has a dark inside room, far more than he loves one who lives in the penthouse, and yet not bother to switch the accommodations. He may choose for special assignments those regarded as the duller tenants or those who previously broke many of the house rules. He will give them the means to carry out the most difficult tasks. As in the case of his natural son, their sufferings may be greatly increased rather than diminished. Yet there will be joy in it too, because the new rule is really a rule of love and the freedom of children replaces the dutifulness of tenants.

The willingness to live by this new law of love is the essence of the heroic, or beatific meekness. Again it involves a docility to reality, but this time to the fullness of reality, to God's whole plan and our own role in it as adopted sons through the grace of Baptism.

Keeping this analogy in mind, then, we can examine the implications of this highest meekness in its several aspects:

1. Meekness toward God.
2. Meekness towards other men.
3. Meekness in imitation of Christ.

MEEKNESS TOWARD GOD

Lots of good people, perhaps the majority of them, resist the new relationship to which they have been raised by Baptism.

They have been given a share in God's own life, but they don't cry, "Abba, Father," as they would if they realized how this adopted sonship could change their own lives. They prefer to go on keeping the rules conscientiously, taking a certain pride, perhaps, in the regularity and order of their little lives, and never doing anything which is foolish in a holy way. They are kind of self-satisfied, almost self-made in their goodness.

To become meek, they will have to become little. They will have to become like little children and let God take over the direction of their lives. He will not lead them to a respectable mediocrity, but to high holiness and a share in God's mysteries. The whole orientation of their lives will be supernatural and unpredictable, instead of neat, cautious and humdrum.

In the spiritual order, to become as a little child is like dying. Unless the grain of wheat falls to the ground and dies, it will never be changed. Unless we *allow* God to remake us, we will never be transformed into His likeness.

Nonresistance

Holiness is much more a matter of self-surrender and nonresistance than of natural effort. That's why meekness is so important, such a decisive virtue. It is not so much a kind of holiness or a manifestation of holiness, as it is the gateway of holiness.

Well-ordered pious people who want to be holy, should therefore concentrate especially on the supernatural means of progress, because these activate the gifts of the Holy Ghost from which meekness derives. The Spirit has to move our spirit before we can cry "Abba, Father." Without concentration on mental prayer and frequent reception of the sacraments, piety peters out into ethical conduct and is in danger of becoming a sort of religious worldliness.

In a way the rebel and the robot are better situated for becoming meek; for though they are in peril of their souls, they are not so threatened by mediocrity or pride.

The tired rebel is like the prodigal son; he longs for home, on any terms. He is shorn of his self-confidence, his desire for the fleshpots and extravagances of materialism. Very likely he is not even in a state of grace; perhaps not even baptized. But his Father is out in the road waiting for him, sees him afar off, and goes to meet him with outstretched arms. The very intensity of the reconciliation and the humility which accompanies it, will allow for a great influx of grace, carrying him well along the path of sanctity. One sometimes sees this phenomenon among converts.

Remedy for Robot

So overwhelmed, by contrast, is the robot with his earthly servitude, that there seems scarcely any room in his life for the divine spark which has been planted in his soul. In fact his mind is so dulled by modern work and recreation that it seems an imposition even to ask him to think much about God.

But this is to reckon without the Father's love, and the resourcefulness of the Holy Ghost working in the Church. The robot has only to listen to the voice of the Church outlining new approaches to spirituality, offering new forms of lay action and apostolate. If he joins the Legion of Mary, becomes a lay missioner, joins a secular institute, goes to Daily Mass and Communion, studies theology, teaches catechism, goes to CFM (Christian Family Movement) meetings and/or does a lot of good Catholic reading, he will be able to make even his routine work and his conformist living the opportunities for serving Christ and incidentally rescuing himself from sub-human irresponsibility.

All this because he, and his pastor, and his Bishop, were meek enough to take their instructions from God speaking through the Church.

MEEKNESS TOWARD MEN

It is only after getting it quite clear in our minds that beatific meekness is directed essentially toward God our Father, and His plans, that we can safely examine how this changes our relations with other men.

Otherwise, we'll get all twisted up with the false doctrines of the day, which profess an exaggerated abeyance before man as such, or before an abstraction called Humanity.

We must also beware of saying too glibly that if God is our Father then other men are our brothers and then hasten to slap them on the backs and call them by their first names in a welter of sentiment about brotherhood.

A safer course is to think of other men as also belonging to the Father. This way we don't take our eyes off God, and our attitude breeds respect and deference rather than overfamiliarity.

"This man," we will say to ourselves, "belongs to my Father, Who has special plans for him, just as He has special plans for me."

From considerations such as these, the meek man develops a delicacy in dealing with other souls. To begin with, his love of the Father creates at least a faint aura of benevolence. But it is because he so consistently refrains from condemning, so habitually withholds judgment and respects the liberty of his associates, that he at least does not interfere with their direct line to the Father and His to them. Maybe at first a meek man can do no more than this, and give good example. It is already quite a bit, and later, if and when he is on fire with charity and full of wisdom, people will stand in line to get his good advice. But meekness is the beginning.

Of course the meek man is well grounded in doctrine and firm about morality, in spite of his deference. He will not let false accusations against the Church go unchallenged, nor will he listen in silence to certain types of conversations. It is in this general area, rather than in his own defense, that his strength will be seen.

Reinforced by Charity

The supernatural meekness of the beatitude will go even further than natural meekness in soothing hierarchical human relationships. The meek man will obey with more good will and command with more gentleness, because his motives have been reinforced by charity. In the natural order, things go better if there is proper docility and meekness all around, or rather, both up and down if the nurse listens to the patient about where it hurts, and the doctor listens to the nurse about the pulse and the blood count and other symptoms, there will be a better diagnosis; and then if the nurse is faithful in carrying out the doctor's orders, and if the patient welcomes the treatment, health will be more quickly restored.

MEEKNESS IN IMITATION

The more heroic our meekness becomes the more it resembles that of Christ, Who told us to learn of Him because He was meek and humble of heart.

As a matter of fact, supernatural meekness is always Christ's meekness, because it results (as do all the beatitudes) from the action of the Gifts of the Holy Ghost in our souls. It is the work of the Holy Ghost to form us in the likeness of Christ, manifesting how Christ would have lived the life of a housewife in Peoria, of a Senator in Washington, of a cripple in Newark. Insofar as we are holy, that is docile under the movement of the Holy Ghost, we are other Christs.

When we begin to be meek, or poor in spirit, or merciful, and look to Christ as our model, we find that He is in a way copying us or setting a pattern that belongs more to us than to Him. For instance since He was God He did not have to obey His parents or pay taxes to the state but He did these things because they are our obligations. And when He seemed to be controlling His temper, it was not really an effort because He had no such problem there as we have.

Explained in Mystery

But as we get holier we begin to resemble the God-man in His divinity, and to do things which can be explained only incorrectly unless they are explained in terms of the Christian mysteries. This is especially true of the meekness of Christ taken as a whole and in its highest manifestations. For meekness is possibly the key quality of Our Lord, bound up with the Incarnation and Redemption.

His meekness, like ours, is sonship. Or rather, it is the other way around. He is the real, natural son, the Second Person of the Trinity, and we are sons by participation in His sonship. He became man only to do the will of His Father and this He did always. So He was always perfectly meek, whether He obeyed His parents or remained behind in Jerusalem; whether He declined to defend Himself or escaped His tormentors; whether He suffered little children or whipped money changers. There is no rule that we can deduce from His conduct about when to turn the other cheek and when not to. He knew His Father's will for Him. We must learn the Father's will for us (where it isn't evident) from the Gift of the Holy Ghost known as Counsel.

But it is when it comes to suffering that we must find explanations more and more in terms of the Redemption mystery.

It was as the will of His Father that Our Lord redeemed us by His Passion and Cross. He was obedient unto death. This supreme act of meekness toward God and men constitutes the redemptive mystery and it cannot be understood wholly from outside. We enter it by living it ourselves.

Once a person enters into the way of holiness, his sufferings are not simply the result of injustice in the old, familiar way, but they become more puzzling.

Should this happen to us, we must keep our eyes on our Father and disregard as much as possible our tormentors, who very likely "know not what they do."

The evil of this world—the *real* evil—is not overcome easily. It is vanquished solely by the merits of Christ, which were won on the Cross in obedience to the Father: His supreme act of meekness.

The best we can do is associate ourselves with this sacrifice, winning not the merits themselves, but something with respect to their distribution; perhaps to those we love, perhaps to our tormentors, perhaps to persons unknown.

Even now, the throngs which surround the throne of the Risen Christ and hail Him as King, unceasingly call Him the Lamb of God. For by His meekness He has taken away the sins of the world and won the right to rule the earth.

This gives us a clue to our own slight share in the reward and the accomplishment which is included in the inheritance promised to the meek.

Also available from
AROUCA PRESS

Meditations for Each Day
Antonio Cardinal Bacci (pbk & hb)

Fraternal Charity
Fr. Benoît Valuy, S.J.

The Epistle of Christ:
Short Sermons for the Sundays of the Year
on Texts from the Epistles
Fr. Michael Andrew Chapman

Our Lady, A Presentation for Beginners
Dom Hubert van Zeller, O.S.B.

A Centenary Meditation on
A Quest for "Purification" Gone Mad
Dr. John C. Rao

Integrity, Volume 1:
The First Year (October–December 1946)
Ed. Carol Jackson, Ed Willock

Christ Wants More:
Ignatian Principles and Ideals on Prayer and Action
Fr. Frank Holland, S.J.

Breaking the Chains of Mediocrity:
Carol Robinson's Collected Works (The Marianist Articles)
Carol Jackson Robinson

AROUCA PRESS REPRINTS:

Dogmatic Theology (Msgr. Van. Noort)
Volume 1: *The True Religion*
Volume 2: *Christ's Church*
Volume 3: *The Sources of Revelation, Divine Faith*

www.ingramcontent.com/pod-product-compliance
Lightning Source LLC
Chambersburg PA
CBHW060402080526
44583CB00012B/434